Robert Watson Frazer

Silent Gods & Sun-Steeped Lands

Robert Watson Frazer

Silent Gods & Sun-Steeped Lands

ISBN/EAN: 9783744752749

Printed in Europe, USA, Canada, Australia, Japan

Cover: Foto ©ninafisch / pixelio.de

More available books at **www.hansebooks.com**

Silent Gods
and
Sun-Steeped Lands

SOME PRESS OPINIONS OF THE FIRST EDITION OF "SILENT GODS & SUN-STEEPED LANDS."

By R. W. FRAZER.

Lecturer in Telugu and Tamil University College and Imperial Institute; Awards from Government of Madras for High Proficiency in Sanskrit, Uriya, and Telugu; Secretary and Principal Librarian, London Institution.

" Such a book could only have been written by a man who is steeped—to borrow a word from his title—to the finger-ends in Indian lore and Indian superstition. . . . The opening story . . . Mr. Frazer tells with such skill and such realism that it is to the Yogi himself we seem to be listening."—Mr. Coulson Kernahan in *The Literary World.*

" These weird, dramatic, half-savage, wholly mystical idylls which Mr. Frazer has woven in this remarkable book."—*Vanity Fair.*

" The author has succeeded in permeating every page with the spirit of India . . . with a spirit and a force which can spring only out of an intimate and scholarly knowledge of history and of modern conditions in the East. Mr. Frazer sets the superstition of 'The Tailless Tiger' in an imaginative episode which enhances greatly its appeal; he weaves a subtle spell, too, around other strange prejudices and beliefs. . . . The illustrations have caught much of the weird charm of the text."—*Academy.*

" A series of stories not only terribly weird and fascinating, not only set in a glamour of Eastern light and shade depicted in poetic language, but containing a distinct underlying current of thought respecting many pressing questions—religious, social, and political —in India of to-day."—*Indian Magazine.*

" Mr. Frazer writes powerfully and well. . . . The tale of the Khond sacrifice is the most striking in the volume, which . . . a most notable contribution to recent Indian fiction."—*Glasgow Herald.*

" There is a weird horror about some of his tales." —*Westminster Gazette.*

" These stories by Mr. R. W. Frazer are a landmark in the history of our literature, for they are the first imaginative treatment by a scholar and a poet of the vast mass of information which has slowly been accumulating about the people and their lives."— *Speaker.*

Silent Gods
&
Sun-Steeped Lands

BY

R. W. FRAZER, LL.B.,
I.C.S., Retired

ILLUSTRATED BY
A. D. M^cCORMICK

London
T FISHER UNWIN
1896

Second Edition.

[*All rights reserved.*]

CONTENTS

		PAGE
1.	THE TAILLESS TIGER	9
2.	THE PEARL OF THE TEMPLE; OR THE WANTON VASANTASĒNĀ	39
3.	THE CRY FROM THE RIVER	61
4.	THE WAIL OF THE WOMAN	93
5.	THE LAST HUMAN SACRIFICE, AND THE ABBÉ LEROUX	107
6.	THE DREAM OF LIFE	167
7.	THE CLOUD MESSENGER (*Adapted from the Sanskrit*)	195

ILLUSTRATIONS

HAVE YOU NO THOUGHT, O DREAMER, THAT IT MAY BE ALL MAYA? . . *Frontispiece*

I WATCHED THE EYES OF THE CHIEF PRIEST AS THEY FOLLOWED HER FAIR FIGURE . *Facing page* 19

SHE FELL SLAIN BEFORE THE IMAGE OF THE GOOD GOD VISHNU . . . . ,, ,, 52

DEATH ALONE COULD FREE HIM ,, ,, 85

DAILY THE POTTER CLANGED HIS CYMBALS . . . ,, ,, 165

THE TAILLESS TIGER.

There was no doubt much truth . . . that the tigers which now infest the wood from Ságar to Devri were of a different kind, . . . in fact, that they were neither more nor less than men turned into tigers, . . . a thing which took place . . . much more often than people were aware of. The only visible difference between the two . . . is that the metamorphosed tiger has no tail, while the ordinary tiger has a very long one.—SLEEMAN, "Rambles and Recollections," vol. i. p. 154 (Constable's Edition, 1893).

THE TAILLESS TIGER.

ONE night I journeyed north, from where the sacred city of Rumbha lies deep hid amid the dense jungles stretching round the southern shores of Lake Chilka, towards the holy city at Puri, within whose portals lies enshrined the shapeless triple form of the great god Jagannāth, Lord of the World. Beneath the arching branches of the massive banyan trees, that lined the roadside in many miles of long stretching avenues, I swiftly rode on, passing the footsore and dust-stained women and children as half-dazed from want of sleep they vainly strove to drag their weary limbs after the men who, intoxicated with the crushed-out juice of the hemp-leaf, hurried on crying out the names of their gods.

Here and there, by the roadside, groups of pilgrims crouched round their camp-fire hastily cooking their food, eager to enter the temple and place their wealth before the priests of Jagannāth, receiving in return the sin-destroying food that had been set before the god.

As the night advanced all lay wrapped in silence, save when the sad moan of the sea-wind swept through the rustling leaves of the trees, or the shrill, grating creak of the rough native carts echoed in the far distance. At times the wild howls of the jackals broke the stillness as they dashed past in fierce packs seeking out the bodies of the fair women and children who had drunk the waters of the wayside tanks and had fallen, slain by the fell cholera.

On I rode in the dense darkness, my horse now and again starting at the weird figures of the pilgrims as, wrapped in white clothes, they lay sleeping round the flickering embers of the dying fires where the gaunt village dogs hungrily fought over the fallen grains of rice.

Suddenly, as the moon shone out from behind the heavy clouds, I saw striding along in the centre of the road a wild, almost unclad, Yogi, his body smeared from head to foot with grey ashes, his long unkempt matted hair hanging down to his waist. As I drew near he seemed not to hear the sound of the horse's footfall, but strode on uttering maniac cries. To all dwellers in India the sight of these half-crazed ascetics is familiar, so I was hurrying past when my horse shied, for the Yogi had plucked a dagger from his waistcloth, and rushed forward crying madly in his own uncouth language, "Gyālopo, Bāhmono, hāni debi!" which may be interpreted "Base-born Brāhman, die!" A blow from the heavy hunting whip I carried in my hand sent the dagger ringing to the ground, whereon the Yogi stood still, gazing up at me in stupid surprise, his thin face, streaked across the forehead with the three broad white lines of Siva, bearing the far-off look of one drunk with opium, while his eyes gleamed red with the maddening hemp juice. Leaning over the neck of my horse I looked down into the wondering eyes that met mine, and cried out in his own language, "Son-in-law of an outcast pariah, dare you raise your hand against an English Sahib?"

"Bābu," pleaded the Yogi, placing

his hands to his forehead in submissive
salutation, "I dreamed that the spirit
of the avenging dead had laid hands
on me to drag me down to the nether
worlds where my soul will soon be
gnawed by foul demons. For have I
not sinned the worst sin the heart of
man knoweth, and how can I escape?
Bābu," he continued, glancing round
in wild fear, "to-day, when the sun
was high in the heavens, I heard the
cry of the wolf, and none has yet heard
the cry of the wolf in the daytime and
lived to see the sunrise. Thrice this
evening I heard the hooting of the
owl, and Bābu," here the Yogi, half
frenzied from fear, drew near and seized
my hand, his long nails sinking into my
flesh, while he continued to speak in
hurried whispers, " saw you not, as you
rode beneath the shadow of the trees,
the tiger that sat by the roadside?"

The Tailless

"No," I replied, looking back uneasily, "I saw no tiger; was it far from here?"

"Bābu, no man may see that tiger and yet live, for it had no tail; why does the Sahib laugh? he knows our language and knows he not that sometimes the spirits of the dead wander about in the form of tigers? By no mortal eye may they be seen till the day of doom approaches, when they appear visible to those who have injured them when living as man, and then they are known, for they have no tails as real tigers have. Bābu, I have seen the tailless tiger, and before the darkness of night rolls away my body will lie mangled in the jungle. As your horse breathed by my side I feared that the accursed Brāhman whom I have slain had returned back from the land of the dead to send my soul to hell."

Tiger &

As I listened to the words of the Yogi I knew not what to do. Before me lay some four hours' journey, and if I delayed probably the last hour would be spent beneath a hot June sun on a jaded horse. Still it was the first time I had ever met a native who professed to have seen a ghost-tiger, though many were the stories I had heard of them. Besides, the Yogi, excited and half-dazed, seemed to have made up his mind that he was to die before sunrise, and as it was but a few hours till dawn I thought that I might keep by his side and see how he would behave when his omens proved false. As I lighted a cheroot I offered him one, but evidently deeming that it would not be polite to accept it, he unravelled some coarse leaves from his long matted hair, and soon, soothed by the smoke, strode along with erect head and gleaming eyes, telling the story of his past in wild, unconnected words.

"Long years ago," he fiercely began, "I sat by the temple gate of Holy Sripati and sold the sandal-wood images of the gods to the pilgrims that passed up and down the sacred hill on which the holy city was built. Bābu, I was but a low-caste seller of idols, and none knew of the wealth I had buried in the house where I dwelt. One day a family of my caste people visited the temple, and among them I saw the face of a maiden that looked fairer than the lotus flowers that shine in the moonlight. Bābu, when a man is born the finger of fate writes on his forehead the course he must run, so—fool that I was!—I declared my wealth to her people, and the maiden, whose eyes shone bright as those of the chakôra-bird, and whose walk was as that of the stately crane,

I WATCHED THE EYES OF THE CHIEF PRIEST AS THEY FOLLOWED HER FAIR FIGURE.

remained behind as my wife. Bābu, I had hidden my wealth, but who can hide the beauty of his wife? As I sold my gods by the temple-gate, I watched the eyes of the chief priest as they followed her fair figure to the tank where she bathed. But was I not a low-caste seller of idols? So one day I had to journey down the hill to buy new images of my gods, and there they kept me waiting, for, Bābu, I speak as a simple man, they whisper in our villages that the power of the priest can stay even the hand of the English rule ; who then was I to know the cunning that crept round about me? But when I returned, my heart grew cold, for I knew not the strange look that lived in the face of my wife. Who can fathom the desire of a man or the love of a woman ? I had watched the eyes of the priest, but had let my wife roam abroad. I dreamed in my rage that the cold eyes of the chief priest met those of my wife, but the tremor of rest ran through my limbs, for I swore that the smile would fade from his face as the slow death crept by his side. When my wife drew nigh I felt that the lips that met mine were cold, and I knew that the love that lit up her heart shed no light on my life, but my eyes laughed bright, for I wished her not to see the rage that surged in my heart. In the night-time, when she slept, dreaming of her lover, I rose and scattered my wealth in the tank near the temple, and as I saw it quickly sink, I swore that so the loathing would sink into the hearts of my wife and her lover ere they died. In the morning I threw ashes on my head and cried aloud that my wealth had been stolen from our house during the night. Eagerly my

Tiger &

wife watched my face as I showed her the broken box where once her rich jewels lay hid, but when she wept and rent her garments, I told her to be comforted, for our love was more than money or jewels, and still lay buried in our hearts beyond the reach of cunning hands. Soon she became soothed, and said she would go south to her people till I gathered more wealth, and my hate grew stronger when I saw that she mourned the loss of her jewels and thought not of the loss of our love. As I sat by her the tears faded from her long eyelashes, and her sloping black eyes flashed with anger while she reviled the poverty of the low-caste seller of idols. I praised the beauty of her face, and told her how the eyes of the priest had followed her as she passed to the well, and how the people who bought my gods had told me that the dancing girls in the temple had ceased to dance before the god, for the chief priest had declared that the grace of the wife of the low-caste seller of idols excelled that of Rumbha the chief of the dancing girls in the heaven of Indra.

"The face of my wife shone strangely as I told her the words of the people, and she braided up her long black hair that fell in heavy folds over her youthful limbs, glowing here and there with the gleam of the polished tusks of the wild roaming elephant. I laughed as I told her how the eyes of the chief priest had followed her as she went to the well, and bade her not to fear, for her beauty would always hold the love of the low-caste seller of idols. Long she mused in doubt, till, seeing the laugh in my eyes, she told me how the chief priest of the temple had gained her love, and she showed me the rich necklace of gold he had given her, which she had hidden in the palm-leaved roof of our house. I bowed my head to hide the hate that surged in my heart, but the laugh grew again in my eyes when I thought how her beauty would soon fade as she waited by the side of the priest for the slow-coming death.

"In the dark of the evening I sat waiting in my house, and the red veins throbbed in my head as my wife stood by the door till her lover drew nigh. I listened as he told her of his love, and came out and bowed down before him as he rose to depart.

"He listened in silence to the story of our loss, and promised to give us wealth if we came that night to the temple. My wife and I waited till all was quiet in the village, and then we stole out and stood in the shade of the

The Tailless

high wall running round the temple till the priest came forth and led us through the wicket of the iron-studded massive gate beneath the many storied gopura towering into the clear starlit sky that gleamed overhead. Hurriedly we passed to the sanctuary of the temple where the light set before the image of the god flickered in the gentle night wind, and the deep silence cast fear on the heart of my wife who crept near my side as I walked on in deep thought, dreading lest I should slay her in my rage and spare her the slow-coming death that would fill her with loathing. Bābu," the Yogi cried, halting, and looking towards me with his wild gleaming eyes, " have you ever climbed the sacred hill of Sripati, and seen the holy temple ? "

" Yes, my friend," I replied, halting to light another cheroot, " few foreigners have ever stood within the portals of that temple save myself. I know not a few of its secrets, and many are the stories I have heard of its chief priest."

"Bābu," whispered the Yogi, coming close to my side, "beneath the holy place in the centre of the temple lies the wealth of ages, and no man knows the way thither, for the chief priest, who held the secret, lay dead before he could tell another. To me alone the secret is known and," here the Yogi gazed with straining eyes into the thick forest that grew down to the road-side, "before the dawn breaks my soul will be wandering to its black abode. To you I will tell the secret of the path to the wealth of the holy temple of Sripati. In the far corner of the temple lies a well hewn out of the solid rock, and down its sides winds a long flight of circling steps. As you turn a wheel close at hand the waters rush down the mountain through the opened sluice at the bottom of the well, and as you once more close the sluice the well is filled from a channel leading from the tank outside the temple. That night the chief priest emptied the waters of the well, and led us down the steps till we reached a door concealed in the damp weed-grown side of the wall. There he lit a torch, and drawing back the door, disclosed to us a long passage which he said led to the chamber where the jewels of the god lay concealed beneath the sanctuary in the centre of the temple, so high that the water could not reach them when the well and the passage were filled. I and my wife swore by the triple thread of the priest that we would never tell of the deeds done that night, and I swore to myself by my scattered wealth and lost love that I alone should live to keep the secret of the strange path whose entrance would ere long lie hid under the silent waters of the well.

"We entered the passage and my wife followed the chief priest up the long flight of steps into the darkness beyond, but I turned and stole back with my heart beating thick in my throat. I held the stone gate in my hand, and watched the shaven head of the chief priest shine in the flaring light of the torch that he carried, while the slender, graceful figure of my wife followed behind, her long black hair rivalling the thick darkness that would soon creep around as she sat by the door listening to the splash of the waters filling the well.

"I laughed wildly when I heard the loud cry of the priest as he turned knowing that I had not followed. I watched the black eyes of my wife gleam with horror as they shone in the red glare of the torch that had fallen at her feet; I rolled the door back to its place and drew the bolt so that no force of man could break it open.

"I sat on the steps, but no sound came through the massive stone, so I ascended and raised the gate admitting the waters of the tank, and waited till I saw that the well was filled, and knew that the rising waters in the passage had driven the priest and my wife back up to the chamber where the jewels lay hid.

"The voice of the watchman sounded in the distance, and the cries of the jackals broke through the morning air as I climbed the high wall of the temple and stole through the deserted streets of the village to my home, where I smeared my body with ashes, and swore that I would not cut the hair of my head till I reached the far-off river of Ganges, and be washed free from the sin of killing a Brāhman.

"In the morning the village watchers came, saying that they had seen me pass with the priest and my wife into the temple during the night, but that I alone had returned. I opened not my mouth when they threatened violence unless I declared the secret of that night, for had I not sworn on the sacred triple thread of a Brāhman that I would not tell where the jewels of the god lay hid? When they saw that I remained silent, they brought me out to the jungle in the dead of night, and tied lighted matches to my fingers, but I laughed as I thought of the dread darkness that crept through the chamber where the priest cried for help.

"The next day they placed me in

the tank so that the waters rose to my lips, and the hot sun poured on my head, till, weary of life, I called them to take me forth, and promised to tell them where my wealth lay hid if they would let me go free. In the night time they dragged up my wealth from the bottom of the tank where I had scattered it, and told me to depart far from the holy hill, so that no man might know how I had escaped.

"So I passed forth from my home, and have wandered to and fro for many weary years from the far south, where the holy bridge of Rāma pierces the black waters, to the far north, where the snowy mountains rise on the boundaries of the world, but still I know no rest, for I have committed the sin of Brāhman murder, and I know that I must be reborn through countless ages in hideous crawling and creeping forms to be crushed by the careless foot of man or destroyed by the myriad hosts of animals that will ever seek to prey on my flesh. But praise be to the gods, the end is at hand, for in the midday I heard the cry of the wolf, thrice I heard the hoot of the owl, and have I not seen the tailless tiger, and before the dawn breaks——"

Somehow, as the droning voice of the Yogi sounded in my ears, I must have gone to sleep, for I remember no more till I was roused by a sudden stumble of my horse. Glancing, half awakened, around I saw that I was alone, the Yogi had vanished as the vision seen in a dream, save that his strange words still rang through my memory.

The night had passed away; down below the road, beyond the dark forest, lay the calm lake of Chilka, glistening in the early rays of the morning sun, while along the narrow strip of land that divided its waters from the far stretching ocean, came rolling the sound of the long sea swell.

Still an hour's journey lay before me, so I hastened on till at length I reached my camp where my tents lay pitched in the shade of a mango grove close to a small village, by the roadside. Tired and jaded, I had hardly drunk the cup of tea my servant held ready for me, when I fell into an uneasy sleep in a long chair in front of my tent dreaming of the wild words of the Yogi.

How long I slept I know not, but when I woke a group of natives stood silent beneath the shade of a distant mango tree, while in front, leaning on a long bamboo stick, waited the village headman, gazing towards my tent.

As I rose and advanced they bowed

down in salutation, and then moving to one side disclosed a long bundle wrapped up in white cloth lying on the ground.

"Mahārāja," said the headman, coming forward and bowing down, "at daybreak, as the village herdsman drove his goats through the jungle near the village, he saw stretched across his path the dead body of a holy man who had strayed from the roadside. Frightened he ran back, and not knowing what to do we brought the body here, so that the ruler might see and no guilt rest on our heads."

As he spoke the two village servants bent down and, drawing away the long white robe, disclosed the emaciated, ash-besmeared body of the Yogi. There he lay, his troubled soul at rest, his face unchanged, save that the wild look of excitement had faded away, the broad white lines on his massive forehead and thick white ashes with which he had smeared himself, to ever keep in his memory the near presence of death, concealing all trace of pallor.

As I watched the still face I noticed that his rosary of thick beads had slipped from his neck and lay stained with blood on the ground beside him. Quickly I looked to the village headman for an explanation. Bending down, he turned the body over and pointed with outstretched finger to the neck of the Yogi while he watched my face. There, a few inches apart, were two wounds just as if an arrow had been shot through the nape of the neck.

Sickened, I moved away, and motioned to the village servants to throw the cloth over the body of the Yogi. Turning to the group of villagers I scanned face after face, and could read there no gleam of intelligence, for they all sat watching in still silence the dead form of the Yogi. Glancing round I met the eyes of the headman who, leaning on his staff, answered back my look of wonder, by slowly saying—

"Mahārāja, there lives no animal in the jungle that could so slay the holy man, save the tiger. Yet when has the tiger relinquished his prey and not torn it in pieces?"

"Said you not," I replied, "that the herdsman came up with his goats; perchance he frightened the tiger away at the moment it killed the Yogi. If you bring the body of the holy man back to the spot where he was found, I will wait near at hand and kill it when it comes in the night-time to prowl in search of its prey."

"Mahārāja," replied the villager,

The Tailless

"we dare not do as you say, for it is the custom of our land to bury the bodies of our holy men before sunset, and never yet have they been burned or longer kept on this earth. Even if we dare do as the protector-of-the poor tells us, yet would he never see the form of that tiger. Mahārāja," he continued, coming close to me, while the villagers shook their heads as they listened to his words, "when the herdsman called us forth from the village, and we stood in the jungle near the roadside, we looked and traced the marks of the feet of the tiger in the forest, and saw how it had sprung on the Yogi, but in the dust we saw no switching of its tail. Mahārāja, you know the signs of the forest, and have told us how no tiger leaves its prey till it has drunk the blood. Mahārāja, we know not the fate that was written on the forehead of the holy man, nor why the spirit of the dead has followed him to our village. We but pray your order that we may bear him forth and bury him according to the custom of our forefathers, so that no guilt may rest upon us. Mahārāja, we are but simple villagers, and know nothing; you are the ruler and will not laugh when we send our report that the holy man was slain by the tailless tiger. Salām, Mahāprabhū, grant us leave to go and bury the holy man."

So saying, the headman motioned to the servants to raise the body of the Yogi, and as they once more bowed, before passing on to the village, I turned towards my tents to wonder how in that land of India, where all is hidden from the gaze of the foreigner, I alone knew the story of the Yogi and the tailless tiger.

THE PEARL OF THE TEMPLE.

"All the temples also maintain troops of dancing girls . . . dedicated to the service of the temples, like the Vestal Virgins of Europe. They were held to be married to the god. . . . Hence they were called the god's slaves."—MONIER-WILLIAMS, "Brahmanism and Hinduism," p. 451.

THE PEARL OF THE TEMPLE.

THE Dravidian people of South India hold no traditions from their forefathers of their ancient primeval home. Though they speak languages allied to those spoken by races living far away to the north of Europe, by the people of Hungary, as well as by aboriginal inhabitants of Australia, yet no man knows when or whence they came to the lands where they now live. No man knows when they learned to bow down before the Aryan gods of North India, or who taught them to build their strangely-carved, many storeyed temples, and to choose out the fairest maidens in their villages to dance before the idols they worship. The foreigner neither knows nor cares; he imagines that the time has already come when the people look no more to their priests, that soon the strange names of their gods will be unheard in the land, and their temples lie silent and deserted. So, perchance, it may be in the future, but one day, as I listened to the story of the good god Vishnu and the wanton Vasantasēnā, the Pearl of the Temple, I learned how in the villages the simple folk still dread the wrath of their gods, and honour their dancing girls who bestow their love where they please.

It was in the days when famine lay sleeping over the land, and the dread cholera mowed down the half-starved folk, that I first journeyed among the people, and heard from their lips the sad, simple story of their lives.

One morning I stood alone on a wide, bleak, treeless plain, watching a herd of antelopes as, startled by the report of my rifle, they fled with frightened leaps far away into the distance. Overhead the sun shed pitiless rays from a brazen sky that for two long years had been crossed by no speck of cloud, giving hope to the people that the rains might fall, fill the rivers, tanks, and dried-up water-channels.

For miles around the waste, black cotton soil gaped in wide fissures, vomiting forth the stifling heat that panted as it surged up, changing the far-off mirage into bewildering, fantastic shapes. I turned to look towards my tents, which lay pitched some five miles distant, in a mango tope by the side of the burning sands of the wide Krishna river, and saw advancing towards me the thin, spare figure of an old man who slowly drove before him two oxen laden with pitchers of goat-skins.

Having eagerly drunk of the cool water he poured into my outstretched hand from his store, I asked him his name and caste, and inquired where his village lay.

"Far away, Mahārāja," he replied, "beneath the palm-trees, the white walls and thatched roofs of my village shine in the sunlight. It now lies empty; no man lives there save myself—I, the village watcher, wait alone for the return of the rains, when those who have fled from the wrath of the raging goddess will again come back to their homes."

The old man sighed as he spoke, and then twisting the tails of his oxen, and driving his goad into their sides, proceeded on his way. As my tents stood

the Temple

too distant to journey back in the heat of the mid-day sun, I followed the old man across the bleak plain, hoping to find shelter in his deserted village till the cool of the evening. As we drew near to the dried rice-fields on the outskirts of the hamlet, I stayed to watch the starved village cattle wander untended along the sides of the empty water-channels, vainly striving to dig out with their heavy horns the green grass roots that had crept deep beneath the parched soil. Close at hand circling groups of unclean vultures danced with long, craning necks and flapping wings round the thin oxen that, too weak to drag their dying bodies out of the reach of the hideous claws and fierce beaks of the well-fed birds, had sunk helpless to the ground.

Sad and sickened I hurried away to join the old man, who had climbed the steep side of the tank, and now stood on the broad bank above. There beneath a solitary drooping palm-tree lay a small white temple containing the symbol of the god, a rude carved stone, daubed with red, before which the women and other simple village folk once bowed down.

The door of the shrine stood open, but within all was neglected, the flower-offerings faded and trampled in the dust. Close at hand was the short square pillar ever to be found in the hamlets of the south, with the sacred Tulsī plant growing on its summit, but the small sweet-scented basil shrub, loved and worshipped by all women of India, long unwatered, was withered and dead.

By the wide uneven stone steps, stretching down to the bed of the tank, where once the village people were wont to bathe, all lay silent ; no longer the quick the Temple &c.

voices were heard pouring forth gossip as in former days, when the village maidens sat happy in the sunshine, or stood knee-deep in the water, their youthful limbs gleaming through their wet white robes, which clung in close folds around them. Walking along the bank we soon gained the high ground on which the small hamlet was built, and, slowly passing through the deserted streets, reached the centre of the village, where, beneath the deep shade of an ancient banyan tree, the old man tied up his oxen, while weary and dazed from the heat of the sun, I seated myself on the crumbling wall of an empty well half-way down which a broken pitcher hung idle at the end of an unused, decaying rope. Around the sun shone bright and weird as if sadly mourning that it alone smiled, while man with his cares and wild passions no longer crept beneath the shade to gaze in wonder at its passing power. It gleamed on the edges of the broad raised verandahs, and cast set shadows on the frail carved pillars which supported the overhanging roofs, leaving in deep gloom the doors and thresholds. Through the rafters, left bare here and there of their thick palm-leaved thatch, it stole within the empty rooms, vainly seeking out those who no more would come forth to greet it with their morning song of praise.

With shaking fingers and nodding head the old man slowly rolled together a few leaves of half-dried tobacco, and as we sat smoking told me the story of the hamlet :

"Father," he began, "we were once happy in the village, the tank and the wells were filled with water, the young green rice glistened in the sun, growing quick in the flooded fields where it had

the Temple

been planted by the busy hands of our women. See, yonder, half-way down the Brāhman street, the white walls of the temple gleam in the sunlight, the lofty pinnacles, carved in cunning devices, rise high, surmounted by the Wheel of Life; but no longer does the protecting god of our village ride out during the night-time on his great eagle, Gāruda, to see that his people sleep safe.

"Then, day and night the wide gates of the temple lay open, and within might be heard the song of the dancing girls as they placed flowers before the image of the god and decked his head with jasmine while they waited for the chief priest. On none was he known to smile save on Vasantasēnā, the Pearl of the Temple, whose dancing princes and rich men had oft travelled from afar to gaze on, bringing rich offerings to the temple, and wealth to the village.

"One night while I watched within the sanctuary, a dread seized me, and my aged limbs trembled, for the eyes of the chief priest flamed with anger and his face grew stern when he saw that Vasantasēnā, the chief of the dancing girls, was not there. The people passed out, but still the chief priest paced to and fro, muttering wrathful words in the holy Sanskrit language, whose sacred sound I, an outcast pariah, had never before been permitted to hear. At length, in harsh tones, he told me to summon Vasantasēnā, so I went forth trembling, for I knew that she danced that night in the house of Gōpāla, a Brāhman from Benares, who had come offering wealth beyond the dream of our poor village, if she would accompany him back to the far north where he dwelt.

"Quickly I went to the house of the Brāhman from Benares, for the behests

the Temple so

of the chief priest brooked no delay; those who opposed him soon died from the pain of the aconite poison or bite of the deadly cobra creeping near as they slept. When I saw Vasantasēnā dancing, in the pride of her beauty and glow of her youth, before Gōpāla, I mingled in the song of the singers the words of the chief priest so that they fell on her ear alone.

"Laughing, she whispered in the ear of Gōpāla, while in jest she sheathed his sharp jewelled dagger in her girdle as she hurried away at the summons she dared not disobey. She hastened to the temple, and her eyes laughed bright as she placed her hand laden with rich jewels on the arm of the priest, who turned his face stern as fate on the eyes that met his.

"Long and low he spoke as she plucked the lotus petals she held in her hand to pieces, or played with the long ruby stones that hung from her ears. Twice her eyes flashed angrily, and she turned to leave the temple, but the priest held her back by whispered words of love. She braided the jasmine flowers in her long black hair, where shone the massive diamond given her that night by Gōpāla, and saw not the rage that surged in the heart of the priest.

"The dead still of the lull that comes before the whirl as the tempest seemed to steal through the temple, as the girl talked on of her new lover, of his wealth and power, but the laugh died on her lips, and her hands remained raised to unfasten the diamond of Gōpāla, as the priest seized the dagger that gleamed in her girdle. Trembling she drew back to rush from the temple, but the life left her limbs, and she fell slain before the image of the good god Vishnu,

SHE FELL SLAIN BEFORE THE IMAGE OF THE GOOD GOD VISHNU.

protector of life, who is ever gentle, shrinking from blood sacrifice. The priest watched the face of the god as I drew near, and turned not as he told me to place the body of the dancing girl by the side of the Brāhman from Benares, so that the guilt might rest on his head. Long I watched near the house of Gōpāla, till weary with waiting for the dancing girl, he sank to sleep, when I crept near and placed the body of his love by his side and drew the dagger from her heart.

"In the early morning I paced through the village, crying out that the night had broken, for the villagers are glad to hear the voice of the watchman telling that all is well. Soon the village awoke, and eager voices cried for the chief men to come forth, for the blood of the dancing girl stained the dagger and garments of the Brāhman from Benares. The course of man's life is written on his forehead, and according to the writing his fate must fall, so Gōpāla bowed his head in silence before the English judge when it was told how he had threatened violence unless the Pearl of the Temple and pride of the village would accompany him to Benares. So he was found guilty of slaying Vasantasēnā, and condemned to death by our rulers, though the native assessors who sat by the side of the English judge would not agree, for they listened not to our evidence, knowing that the chief priest had somehow set snares about Gōpāla so that he might die. But, praise be to Vishnu, he died not by the hand of the hangman, for the power of a Brāhman holds sway within the prison gates which swung open in the dead of night to let Gōpāla steal forth to seek the dancing girls who waited for him in Benares.

the Temple

"Father, that night, when the dancing girl lay dead in the temple, the good god Vishnu went forth from the village mourning for the spilt blood of his servant Vasantasēnā, and there was none left to protect us. Though the chief priest performed the sacred rites for the purification of the temple, where never till Vasantasēnā lay dead had aught save sweet scents and fair flowers been strewed, his limbs grew numb and his eyes sank deep when one night the dread cholera crept near. They carried him out and laid him to rest by the running waters of the river, but the wrath of the fierce goddess surged in his veins and shook his frame, till weary of life his soul struggled out to seek the god he had dishonoured. The same morning the pains of death passed into the limbs of the dancing girls as six of them sang their sad song of sorrow, seated in the street before the abode of Vasantasēnā, and the same flame wafted the souls of the chief priest and the six women to the heaven of Indra.

"The wide Brāhman street stretching in front of us, which once echoed with the sacred sound of the Sanskrit sloka, is now empty and deserted, for one by one the holy men walked the path of Yama the Messenger of Death. Outside the village, as we passed the house of the potter, saw you not the half-moulded water-pot still standing dry on the centre of the wheel which whirls no longer? Father, the hand that moulded the clay was numbed and the voice that sang as the shape took form moaned but for a moment as the tremor of death passed over the threshold. In days gone by I have often stood in the midday heat before the house of the potter and watched him mould his clay, wondering if the gods mould the hearts of men with as cunning hands. Who knows? The gods have made us, and we dare not wonder at their handiwork. The ryots who spread the water in the fields and sowed the seeds that woke to life lay dead before the rice was ready for reaping. No man knows how the gods work; it were better perhaps the rice should grow and the men die.

"Here is my horoscope cunningly devised by the astrologer, who read my fate in the stars and saw not the writing that foretold his own end. All have died, even the Yogi who fasted and defiled the body he dreaded to part with when the messenger of death came to call his soul away.

"For long days in the village we sat waiting for death, each thinking for himself. The village doctor hastened round and gathered up wealth; it now lies by him in the rushes where the jackals buried him. As the people died one by one, the weaver still sang as he quickly shot the shuttle with the weft through the warp, while his wife sat spinning by his side. But one day he went weeping to gather up the silk and carry the spindle and spinning-wheel to the side of his wife, when weary with the weight of the water-pot she bore from the well, she came home to die. Now the half-weaved cloth lies idle on the loom before the house where they once lived.

"Seeing the village grow empty, the merchants gathered up their merchandise and fled from the wrath of the raging goddess, who slew them in the highways, and drank up their life as they slept by the roadside.

"Does the Protector of the Poor ask who is the raging goddess? Knows he not the fierce Kālī, who wears a necklace of dead men's skulls and a girdle of dead men's hands, who once danced on the body of her husband, the three-eyed Siva, and ever since rides through the land, seated on the spotted tiger, seeking to lick up the life of the living with her red, lolling tongue. She has cursed the waters of our wells, and swept the clouds from the skies. I alone live, for I drink not the sweet waters of the wells ; in the night-time I steal out and fill my goatskins from the stream that springs up in the far-off river. But soon, Father, the favour of Vishnu will shine again, for before night-time the roar of the thunder will be heard and the flash of the lightning will be seen as the good god Indra pours down the rain and the dread goddess Kālī rides forth from the village."

As the old man spoke, he pointed to the dark clouds that now rolled heavily

The Pearl of the Temple

up along the horizon. Far overhead the rushing wind chased the rugged fleece clouds across the pale grey sky. Soon in the distance the tall palm-trees bowed before the raging storm, while through the village swept the scattered straw from the roof-tops, mingled with the driving dust and sweet scent of the coming rain, through which I rode back to my tents by the side of the sands of the wide Krishna river.

THE CRY FROM THE RIVER.

There is one world-wide and inveterate superstition belonging to the sacrificial class—of which we have many vestiges in India—it is the belief that a building can be made strong, can be prevented from falling, by burying alive some one, usually a child, under its foundation.—LYALL, SIR ALFRED, "Natural Religion in India," Rede Lecture, 1891, p. 47.

THE CRY FROM THE RIVER.

EVERY river in India, from its birth in the lonely mountains above the Ghauts, along its wild career through the fertile plains, till it sullenly bursts over the bar of sand impeding its passage to the sea, bears stories strange and weird of the sages, saints and priests of old who blessed or cursed the flowing waters as the fancy took them.

To many is known the black Rākshakuliya as it rolls past the ancient town Aloka. Round the buttresses of the nine-spanned bridge that locks its banks together it whirls and swishes its raging waters ever sadly murmuring o'er and o'er again the story of the two fair women whose love lies chilled to death in its cold embrace.

One night, when the rains of the south-west monsoon hurried down the streams from the mountain tops, the village watchers of Aloka sent word to my camp saying that their homes lay in danger from the river's flood.

As I rode through the village to the river bank the people, with bowed heads and folded hands, crowded round crying out that since the bridge lower down the river had been built the pent-up waters had yearly swept closer in on their houses and temple. Loudly they prayed that orders should be given to make the river banks safe, for it had ever been the custom of their ancient rulers to protect the poor and see that no harm came to the village.

However, I knew too well that many

were the reports that would have to be prepared, and many the days that must elapse before the Government would undertake the work, so I shortly told the people that nothing could be done till the water subsided, and warned the headman that if in the night-time the river rose higher, the land on which the village temple and surrounding huts stood lay in danger of being swept away by the monsoon flood.

As I spoke the temple priest, an aged Brahmān, standing tall and erect with folded arms, his sharp features deeply marked from small-pox, fixed his small cunning eyes, with half-concealed contempt, on mine, and asked in haughty tones—

"The temple of Siva has stood here since the days of my forefathers. They and I have lived on the lands, now standing in my name in the Government

Records, set apart for the service of the god. Has not the temple been here for ages the sole temple of the village, why then should it now be in danger?"

"I know nothing of the rich lands you and your forefathers have eaten," I carelessly replied, not liking the look nor the tone of the priest. "See you not for yourself how the river has crept in, washing the banks away from above and below the temple? Were it not for the long roots of the toppling trees near the stream, the sandy bank would ere now have been swept away."

"The banks of the river not five years ago stood far away from the temple; house after house, tree after tree, has fallen away, yet never have the waters come over the threshold of the abode of the gods, why now should they come nearer?" asked the priest in the same defiant voice.

the River &

"Proud Brāhman priest," I answered back in his own language, for till now we had spoken in English, which he had learned well. "See you not the nine-spanned bridge but a man's cry down the river? Since the day that bridge was built the waters, changed in their course, have come rolling in here on your village, and are even now creeping beneath the very foundations of the temple."

As I spoke I wondered at the strange change that came over the scowling face of the priest. It grew pale and his eyes flashed fiercely. His lips moved quickly while he muttered rapid words, but as he raised his clenched hand and seemed about to speak he checked himself, and drawing his white robe round his arms hastened away from the river's bank down the long village street. The crowd slowly followed, passing away one by one with downcast looks.

The Cry from

Left alone with my syce I rode along the banks of the river towards the bridge. Hardly had I ridden half the distance before the rain increased till it fell in heavy sheets, while the gleam of each lightning flash dashed along the edges of the thick clouds only to fade away and leave the heavens dull and sullen. As my horse stumbled on through the soft sand, I saw in the distance an ancient, dismantled, two-storeyed mansion, standing out clear on the river's bank as the lightning flashed bright. Riding near I gazed with wonder at the massive pillars and broad staircase leading to the upper storey, all built with marble brought from the west to satisfy the lordly whim of some former owner. In front lay the neglected remains of a spacious garden where the splashing rain now collected in pools and filled up the basins of ruined fountains. Dismounting, I walked with heavy boots and clanking spurs round the lower verandah, where the wind came whistling through the tattered remains of the close cane blinds which once served as a shade. Every door was closely locked, and as I strode on, my footsteps echoing hollow in the strange stillness, innumerable bats flew out from the cornices and nooks, rousing, by the soft flapping of their wings, ghostly thoughts that the place was haunted by unclean spirits. Fearing that the dreaded cobra and other snakes might have sought refuge from the rains in the dry stone pavement, I hastened out and ascended the broad steps leading from the garden to the storey above.

There all seemed silent and deserted.

As I stood undecided on the top of the staircase, I saw through the closed venetian shutters of a window facing the river the gleam of a faint light. My footsteps must have been heard, for the broad double door of the room was slowly opened, and a tall Englishman with straggling black beard, wearing slip-shod boots and shirt unbuttoned at the throat, stood gazing at me with vacant look as if he were drunk or dazed.

In answer to the words of apology I stammered forth for my intrusion his replies were few, coming from his lips mechanically, as though he took no interest either in my presence or remarks.

"Yes, I might have a light for my cheroot. Sorry there was nothing in the house to offer me. He never went out now. Yes, he would have a cheroot; glad to get one, as he could only get native tobacco from the village. Would bring out a chair for me, and sit himself

the River

on the parapet. No, he did not mind the rain, had lived a long time in the country and was used to it."

As he did not seem inclined to talk further, I sat watching him, hoping that soon the rains would cease, so that I might hasten back to my camp. At times he stood gazing down over the parapet into the river, where the raging waters rushed past the side of the house. At times he walked aimlessly up and down the verandah, his hands in his pockets, his head sunk deep on his breast, unheeding the incessant gleam of the lightning in which the white polished walls of the house shone as though it were bright day.

Suddenly a wild shriek, rising above the rush of the storm and whirl of the waters, broke the stillness of the place, echoing down the wide verandah.

Again and again the cry was repeated, each time sounding nearer and nearer, till the lightning bursting forth disclosed the erect figure of the priest I had seen in the village. Up the centre of the steps he strode, cries of rage and passion broke from his lips as his eyes met those of the Englishman, whom he seized by the arm, dragged to the edge of the verandah facing the river, and, pointing to where the swollen waters hurled themselves against the sides and piers of the bridge, hoarsely shrieked—

"May the wrath of the gods fall heavy on your head, may your soul ever wander unappeased about your accursed bridge. See, down in the village the lights flit to and fro round the temple near which the waters now rush, threatening ruin. For ten long years I have waited the summons of the god, shed daily before him the blood of

the River

goats, poured forth wealth at his feet, brought dancing girls from afar to sing his praise, but the mighty Siva slept satisfied with the blood and love of the two victims I placed in his strong arms. To-night, as I stood watching the image in the temple, I saw the deadly cobra, that bears the foot of Vishnu on its head, crawl from the mouth of the god, overturn the sacred offerings and flickering fire, so that I knew the dread god Siva slumbered no longer and that he had gone forth threatening woes, disease and pestilence unless appeased with the blood he loves.

"The cry that you and I have twice heard came again last night from the river and sounded through the village, telling that the spirits of the dead move about wailing the fate that hangs over those soon to join them in the rolling tide. Now let the dread god select whom he chooses, and may you and your black bridge be swept far away so that the village again be in peace. Once more, mighty Lord of the Three Spaces and Times, declare your wishes; the blood of my blood lies cold in the dread depths of the river, and the love of the foreigner lies quenched on the cold bosom of its waters. Thrice have I prayed for your wrath to fall on his head; stretch forth your dread hand and sweep the accursed Mleccha, who has polluted the Aryan blood, and his bridge from off the land."

The priest paused to gaze down on the swollen river, now rising higher and higher, till at length its water lapped over the basement of the house. Long and eagerly he listened to the loud whirl and roar as if he expected a voice to come from the flood. Raising his eyes he looked in anger at the bridge that loomed indistinctly through the surrounding darkness, and then turned to listen to the confused cries that came from the villagers who flitted to and fro bearing lights near the temple round which the raging waters now swept. As the Englishman drew back from the edge, dazed by the noise and blinding lightning, increasing in intensity and brightness with every peal of thunder, the priest followed, and drawing him again towards the parapet of the verandah, continued in frenzied tones—

"Deem not that you can escape from the wrath of the gods once they have paused to listen to the prayers of a Brāhman, and heard his curse go forth on those who do evil. Listen now to what my power has worked in the past and judge if the gods hearken not to my call.

"Twice ten long years ago you first

came to our village. You grew in wealth as you bought the crops and sold them abroad, and the willing hands of our people built you this house, for to all you seemed just and generous. You had grown to live among us as one of our race, so, according to our customs, I, the chief priest, was besought to declare an auspicious day for the consecration of your new home, for none of our people would enter till the signs were declared favourable. You freely poured forth wealth to feast the gods and temple servants, still the stars and omens were adverse, so, in spite of your prayers and entreaties, I refused to perform the sacred rites. At length one day, moved to wrath by your importunities and insults, I called down the anger of the gods on you and all your works. When the people heard my wrathful words, they told me of your evil deeds, how you had gained the love of my daughter doomed to widowhood through the death of her affianced husband, how you had trampled on our religion and caste, daring to hope that a woman descended from a race sprung from the gods might be yours.

" Fool ! listen now to what a Brāhman's pride and curse can work. You entered your house, your wealth broke down the religious scruples of the people, but while the great god Siva slept I waited, knowing that the curse and the power of a Brāhman never fell futile. My daughter—outcast from her religion and people—sat alone pining for a sinful, polluted love, and a false message told you that she was dead. She died not then, for I had sworn that she should die by the hand that had robbed her of honour here and hope hereafter. Mad with grief and sorrow, you quitted this land for your own, and returned one year afterwards full of new hopes. Vainly you sought to bridge the sacred river, but the great god Siva scattered your walls in the waters. Six times you laid your foundations, six times they were swept away. The people then listened to my voice and prayed you to hearken to the wishes of the gods, and to call forth the village priest to perform the sacred rites, else the foundation stone could not stand. You consented, and in the night-time I concealed your love and her child in a hollow dug out in the dry bed of the river, and I told the people that there the foundations must first be laid. You laughed as you lowered the stone that condemned them to a living tomb, for you never knew that the cries of your loved one were drowned by my song of praise, giving thanks to the gods that the curse of a

Brāhman had not fallen in vain. Fool, the bosom of the waters held my only offspring sacrificed to the outraged pride of a Brāhman, but my revenge was not complete.

"Day by day I kneeled before the god in the temple praying for an ampler and fuller revenge that would sink into the inmost recesses of your heart. Your most trusted servants were in my pay and would have sacrificed all to do my behests, but I wanted not your life, I wished you to live and eat the fruits of the deeds you had done.

"I heard that a woman was coming from your own country to gain the love that had polluted our race. The letters you received and the letters you wrote were opened and read by the gleam of the light that shone before the god in the temple; and on the boat that bore your love from the black sea waters up the sacred river that runs before us, my power held sway and the steersman was sworn to ruin your hopes as you reached out your hands to grasp them. You knew not that I stood by as you watched the smoke rise above the horizon, telling that the love you hoped to grasp once more was being rapidly carried nearer. Do you remember how the rain fell and the waters rose as the boat came in view with the pale-faced English maiden standing at the bow, how the torrent came rushing from the mountain tops and the boat swung round and drifted to the bridge? I laughed as I heard you cry out wildly to the boatmen, and I chanted hymns of praise to the gods of the waters as you fell on your knees, praying for the help that came not. I gathered up my raiment together as I passed out of the midst of the crowd, when the crash and wild shriek came telling that your love and hopes were again shattered on the pier, held firm by the arms of the woman you had buried beneath it. In the pride of my victory I scattered the wealth hoarded up by my forefathers for generations, thwarted your plans, ruined your endeavours, brought your proud head to bow where you had been master, and have lived to see you an outcast beggar in the ruined house that once rang with your laugh of mockery over the village Brāhman and his anger."

As the Brāhman spoke the Englishman swayed to and fro, his ashy pale face, from which now all traces of the havoc wrought by the foul drink had passed, glaring in the incessant flashes of lightning as that of one who had risen from the grave. Twice he prepared to hurl himself on the weird, thin figure that stood erect and vaunting before him, twice the set features of the Brāhman seemed as if they owned a power not born of this world and held him back.

With gleaming eyes and erect head the priest turned and strode away, down the steps, along the avenue of palm-trees leading from the house to the village, crying with still, clear voice to the protecting god of his race, "Om! Om! Hari, Om."

Long I stood gazing after the priest, astounded at the wild words he had spoken. As I looked once more towards the lone Englishman, I saw that he leaned far over the parapet listening to the distant cries from the village, now faintly heard amid the rush of the waters and moan of the wind. Following his eager gaze, I fancied that

the River

I saw the flickering lights near the temple come towards us, moving down the stream.

Suddenly a wild shriek—it was the voice of the priest—burst from the midst of the seething waters as the lights came rushing past the house. The thunder rang from heaven to earth, the lightning lit up the sky, showing that a raft of hewn timber, broken from its moorings in the higher reaches of the river, had been hurled against the jutting bank, which it now swept, with temple, priest, and people, down the river towards the ill-fated bridge. There it struck, damming up the waters till the bridge gave way. The thunder rolled but to drown the crash of the falling masonry and the wild cries of the people hurled to and fro in the seething waters. One more flash of lightning burst forth as the escaping waters rushed forwards, sweeping before them their devastating burden. Slowly the wind became hushed and the sullen roar of the thunder faded in the distance, while the lightning played in a faint and fitful gleam over the thick darkness that lay sleeping on the black river. The storm was quickly passing, and as with beating heart and trembling lips I turned to call for help, I saw that the Englishman had disappeared. Still the dim light shone from the half-opened door. In the room beyond he sat, his head bowed down on a table, his hand stretched out grasping an empty tumbler, near which stood a bottle like those sold in the villages of India to hold the vile spirit distilled from the opium-poisoned juice of the palm-trees. I would have entered and spoken, but I saw that

the River

before him lay no future ; death alone could free him from the bonds that bound him hand and foot to his fate, for beside him stood a native woman with face bent down, but whose small, thin hand and heavy gold jewels told me that it was one who had known him in the days of his wealth and still clung to his side.

I hastened away to join the villagers, who now with loud cries hurried past the house, but when we reached the bridge the swollen waters ran high, and nought could be seen but the black, rolling flood.

Early the next morning I had to travel away from the village to visit other towns in the district, where the heavy monsoon rains had spread ruin far and wide. Two years elapsed before I again visited the village of Aloka.

The Cry from

Riding in late one moonlit evening I learned that my servants had placed my cot and camp furniture in the very room in the ancient mansion where once the strange, lonely Englishman lived. As I dismounted at the foot of the wide staircase I noticed that the house and all around was in the same desolate, deserted condition as of old.

Ascending to the verandah above, I looked down once more on the black Rākshakuliya to watch the gleam of the moonlight flit on the still waters of the wide flowing river. In the distance still loomed the bridge, six arches standing, three on each side near the banks, the centre three gone, never having been rebuilt since they had given way before the monsoon flood. As the wild words of the Brāhman priest rose in my memory I dreaded to look round, for a weird fancy seized me that the Englishman stood close at hand, gazing towards the still waters below, on the sad faces of the two women swept from his side by the pride of race and fanatic power of superstition.

Again I pictured to myself the peaceful country village in England where perhaps free from all ties, but heart-broken and footsore, he now journeyed alone along some well-known road running past a rustic, moss-grown church, standing in the midst of the sad memorials of those among whom he longed to be at rest. Else perchance, with bitter heart and weary mind he still wandered, like many another ruined soul of his race, through the peaceful villages of India, begging for the vile drink the people gladly gave him when he promised to remove his hated presence from their midst. As I sat dreaming I was suddenly roused by hearing a light footfall and tinkle of a woman's jewels close by my side.

There stood a fair dancing girl, whom I guessed from her figure to be the woman I had seen before in the room, standing by the side of the Englishman.

As I turned and my face shone bright in the moonlight, she smiled, and raising her heavily bejewelled hands to her forehead, lisped out in the soft, pleading tones of her caste—

"Mahārāja, I was in fear when I saw you sitting here alone, for I fancied that the Englishman who built the house and bridge had come back to the land of the living."

"Sister," I answered, rising, "what brings you here? The house is empty, I alone sleep here for the night."

"Mahārāja," she said, coming nearer,

the River

"fear you not to be here alone? They say in our village that the spirit of the Englishman still wanders about, and at times when the waters come rushing from the mountain tops, leaping like wild horses, the sound of his voice may be heard crying from the waters."

"Is, then, the Englishman dead?" I asked in anxious curiosity.

"Mahārāja, I know not; one night some two years ago I sat by his side, for of the great wealth he had stored I was then all that was left to him. I had eaten of his wealth in days gone by, so I left him not when the people held aloof. That night I heard him speak angry words with the chief priest, who, I am glad, was swept away in the river, for when afterwards I spoke words of love to the Englishman, he drove me from his side and bade me never more come near the house."

"Why, then, have you come here to-night?" I said, noticing that the dancing girl wept and drew her white robe round her face. "Tell me, sister, what became of the Englishman?"

"Brother," she replied, holding my hand as she gazed in fear into the surrounding darkness, "that night I slept in the far verandah of the house. Once I woke in fear, for the cry that is ever since heard when the waters come rushing down from the mountains rang through the house. I hurried round the verandah and looked in each room, but the Englishman had vanished, and ever since his spirit wanders about near at hand. So weekly I come here bringing cigars and brandy to place on the verandah, so that his soul may not go away unappeased. Mahārāja, when the grey morning creeps up from beyond the far-off horizon, be not afraid

<u>the River</u> ❦

if you hear the cry from the river creep round the verandah, for it is but the wail of the soul of the Englishman going forth to the river below. Salām, Mahārāja, bid your servants not to touch the offerings I leave here. I will come again in the morning to know if you have heard the cry from the river."

THE WAIL OF THE WOMAN.

It is calculated that in India one woman in five is a widow; of these a very large proportion must be women who, having been betrothed any time between the cradle and ten years of age, have become widows without ever having been wives. . . . It is only by the education and elevation of women that any change can come over the feeling of the people with regard to marriage.—DUFFERIN AND AVA, MARCHIONESS OF, *Nineteenth Century*.

Widow marriage among the high caste people will not for a long time become an approved custom. The old idea is too deeply rooted in the heart of society to be soon removed. Secondly, there are not many men who will boldly come forward and marry widows.—RAMABAI, "The High-Caste Hindu Widow," p. 51.

THE WAIL OF THE WOMAN.

THE wide Brāhman street in the village of Kāmapuram lay deserted and silent beneath the burning rays of a mid-day sun, for the men and women had gone forth in the pride of their caste to the English Court House to laugh at the laws of their rulers.

Inside the Court a young Brāhman widow, her fair face hidden in the folds of her long white robe, stood before the pale-faced English judge who wearily gazed now and then at the slow-swinging punkah that fitfully moved the stifling air in hot blasts over a long table below, where the native Brāhman pleaders sat cold and immovable. By the side of the judge stood a native clerk, who, with droning voice, read out the charge, telling how the woman had cast herself and her child into the well near the village temple, and how, though the woman had been saved, her child lay dead.

The Court became still, and the people bowed down as her father—a proud Brāhman priest, tracing back his descent from the Vedic sages of old—came forward, and stood erect and haughty, dreading lest even his white robes should be contaminated by the low-caste English officials. Defiant and calm he gave witness that his daughter, widowed from her youth, had broken the laws of their caste, and following the law of the foreigner had married one who dared to think that he could defy the wrath of the gods. He then told how her husband, the outcast breaker of the laws of his race, had died, and how his daughter had thrown herself and her child into the well in front of his house.

When he ceased the slow, monotonous voice of the native clerk sounded through the Court as he read the report of the English doctor, declaring that the child had been cast into the well after the life had gone from its limbs, and that it had died from the aconite poison found concealed in the house of the Brāhman priest.

As the woman listened to the words of the report, and saw the stern face of her father grow pale, she threw the white robe from her head and her eyes gleamed with rage.

The Court became hushed as the English judge leaned forward and bade her stand by his side and fear not to tell the truth.

"I am a woman," she said, drawing the white robe once more round her head, "and know nothing; how can I speak? Yet the love of my husband and child cries in my heart; wild words rush to my lips, and I would that their death were avenged ere I die. Once I was happy as a child, and ran free through the village, till one day I was told that my affianced husband, whom I had never seen, lay dead, and that I must henceforth live alone and mourn all the days of my life. I remember how I shuddered when, according to the custom of our race, the outcast wife of the village barber was hastily summoned to shave the long black hair from my head, and gather the jewels from my ears, and break the bracelets on my arm, while my mother sat by my side and bitterly cursed the fate that had fallen on our family. For five long years I mourned in silence, and patiently bore the stern looks of my father and my mother's hate which day by day grew deeper as she remembered how her only child had been born unlucky.

"When the dancing-girls passed down the busy sun-lit streets singing their glad songs of welcome before the happy bride I sat alone, for I knew that all looked with loathing on the woman whom death had forgotten. So the weary days wandered on, till there came to our village a Brāhman who had been outcast from his own people, for he had crossed the black waters of the far-stretching sea, and had eaten with the foreigners who have no fear in their hearts, and care not for the power of caste, or the wild, silent passion that rages in the hearts of the people whose gods they have broken in pieces.

"In secret we wandered together

through the deep grove by the side of the river, where the painted butterflies flitted round the thick clustering blossoms of the sweet scented babool-trees, and the dark tamarind topes cast a deep shade over the hot sand, till weary with the heat of the day we sank to dream of the happy life that throbbed all around.

"For years the weary nights had passed slowly and sadly, and I woke in the mornings to wash the tears from my eyes, but now, as I lay awake under the open verandah of our home, I watched the far-off heavens where the stars laughed music back to my soul while I dreamed that the eyes of my beloved kept watch close beside me.

"When I closed my eyes to seek sleep, my thoughts wandered back to the cool sedges by the side of the slow-flowing waters of the wide river near the grove where we had sat together in the sunshine, breathing the heavy perfume of the long trailing jasmine. So the sorrow went forth from my heart, and the laugh grew again on my lips, and as I looked in the water I loved to think that my lover had not lied when he spoke of my beauty. But my soul grew dead when I watched the fair moon, the Mother of Lovers, whose glance fell cold on the outcast widow, for I remembered the wild words my father had wrathfully uttered when my mother told him of the love that had grown in my heart.

"One day, when the warm wind blew over the hot sands of the river, I went to the grove and waited for my lover, who came smiling, not seeing that I sat silent. He laughed at the words of my father, and told me how the law of the Rāj, stronger than the law of caste, had declared that a widow might marry, and he prayed me to come forth from my people and live by his side.

"I consented, and we were married according to the laws of the Rāj; but as we passed home the streets were deserted, and my father sat by the temple gates and cast dust on his head, praying that the curse of a Brāhman might fall heavy on the head that had defied the wrath of the gods, and had brought his pride low before the people.

"The laws of the caste are strong, and they declare that no widow of our race may re-marry, so we were not allowed to draw water from the well, or receive fire from the house of any caste man; but we laughed in the joy of our youth at the anger of the people and the wrath of my father.

"So the days of a happy year passed by and our child was born. One day when my husband returned home, the smile had faded from his face, for he had seen my father, who still sat daily by the temple gates, having refused to enter into his house or eat with his own people till the stain was removed from his race. Who can stand long alone? We sat silent that evening, and ate not; but my husband drank of the milk they brought him from the village; and in the night time he cried aloud that the sight had faded from his eyes, and that he dreaded to face the gods he had forgotten. I gave him water to quench the fire that burned in his throat, but the life fled from his lips as I watched alone by his side.

"In the morning my mother came and took my child and bade me go bathe as a widow in the waters of the river, and there I sat mourning as the quick flame carried the soul of my husband to the abode of the gods. When I returned home I found that my child lay dead; so I carried it to the well by the side of the temple, for I could not leave it alone when I went forth to seek the soul of my husband, as it wearily waited on its lone journey through the cold realms of death.

"I am a woman, and cannot tell what all these things may mean. My husband has told me that the law of the Rāj is strong, and that the God of your people is mighty; but I know that the laws of the caste strike deep, and that the gods of our people are many. Will the law of the Rāj now lay hands on those who rule the law of the caste and make the gods of the people?"

The English judge wrote on, and his pale face turned not as the woman fell and placed her hands on his feet. The widow was free to go where she would, for the law knew not of her cries and tears; but her father lay dead ere the rains had ceased.

* * * *

The story is old; but still in the land of India, though the sun shines bright and the soft, warm wind lulls the soul to rest as it wantonly waits for the eyes that love and the voice that whispers as the dreams drift past, woes and wails of years, tears and moans untold rise unheard to the heavens above, for the woman that sins must die that the will of the man may live.

THE LAST HUMAN SACRIFICE
AND THE ABBÉ LEROUX.

The best known cases of human sacrifices, systematically offered to insure good crops, is supplied by the Khonds, or Kandhs, another Dravidian race. . . . The sacrifices were offered to Tari Pennu or Bera Pennu. . . . The victim or Meriah was acceptable to the goddess only if it had been purchased, or had been born a victim, . . . the flesh and ashes of the victim were believed to be endowed with a magical or physical power of fertilising the land. The same intrinsic power was ascribed to the blood and tears of the Meriah, his blood causing the redness of the turmeric and his tears producing rain.—FRAZER, J. G., "The Golden Bough," vol. i. pp. 384-390.

The Kharwars, since adopting Hinduism, performed human sacrifices to Káli. . . . The same was the case with the Bhuiyas, Khánds and Mundas.—CROOKE, "Popular Religion and Folklore in North India," p. 296.

The low castes pour out the lives of countless goats at the feet of the terrible Káli, and until lately, in time of pestilence and famine, tried in their despair to appease the relentless goddess by human blood. During the dearth of 1866, in a temple to Káli, a body was found with his neck cut. . . . In another temple at Húglí (a railway station only 25 miles from Calcutta) the head was left before the idol decorated with flowers. Such cases are the survivals of the regular system of human sacrifices which we . . . see among the non-Aryan tribes.—HUNTER, SIR W. W., "The Indian Empire," p. 264.

THE LAST HUMAN SACRIFICE AND THE ABBÉ LEROUX.

I.

AMID the deep recesses of the forest-clad mountain slopes, forming the steep barrier between the Highlands of Central India and the lowland plains, lie hid away from all save the stray traveller strange wild scenes of primeval grandeur. Nature, gloomy and mysterious, holds there eternal revel.

The days blaze bright with tropical sunshine, the nights clear and chill strew the sedges of the marshes with white hoar frost. The streams, rippling clear

The Last Human Sacrifice

as translucent silver, bear the poisoned seeds of deadly fever. Beneath tall forest trees creeps the dank, moist atmosphere, bearing lazily through the thick tangled undergrowth its heavy taint of malaria.

The crow of the gaudy-coloured jungle cock, the cry of the peacock, and quick bark of the tiny, slender barking deer alone, now and then, break the sad, weird silence of the lonely forests. The tall samber deer, with long branching antlers, keep watch and ward in the shaded glens over the timid does and their fawns; the fierce cheetah and black-skinned panther prowl through the grass which grows on the mountain side higher than the height of a tall man; the gliding trails of serpents of huge girth may be traced across the sands of the dry streams, the man-eating tiger wanders about slaying between

and the Abbé Leroux

sunset and sunrise belated travellers who journey on mountain tracks separated by some eighty miles of almost impenetrable forest. At times the tinkling bells of the pack bullocks of Brinjāri gipsies, the ancient carriers in many lands, sound up the sides of the ghauts, as the long caravans pass through the forests bearing salts and merchandise from the sea-coast to the rich valleys away towards the West. As caravan meets caravan the gipsy women, brilliantly arrayed in thick raiment of many colours, with massive silver bangles on their arms, and long heavy gold chains and bells hanging from their ears, dismount hastily from their asses and oxen, fall with loud cries on each other's necks, then crouch down with heads buried in their hands weeping and moaning as they remember the lonely terrors of the land through which they

The Last Human Sacrifice

journey, their kinship and long separation, while the men sit silent, gazing at each other with sullen brows, and the tall, gaunt dogs, guardians of the gipsy camp at night-time, attack each other in fierce anger.

At length the caravans separate to continue their course, the one down the mountain path to the distant sea, the other to the wild country above the ghauts where the Khonds, a race some 100,000 in number, haveg rouped themselves together in hamlets to plough and till the soil cleared here and there by fire of the forest trees and thick jungle.

In these rich valleys hid among the hills, the savage tribes live fierce and untamed, simple and truthful, knowing nothing of the blessings or curses of civilisation, for the lowland trader has not yet taught them how to lie. Keen of hearing and quick of sight they watch the forest signs, track the wounded tiger and mark down the lairs of the brute beasts with unfailing instinct. In the hot weather they roam through the jungle in search of food, or else, intoxicated from the crushed-out juice of the mohwa flower and fermented sap of the stately sago-palm, rest beneath the shade of the trees, their long-handled battle-axes, bows and arrows ever lying ready for use to avenge a real or imaginary wrong.

Well it is that the strong arm of the English rule metes out speedy and stern justice to the offender who unjustly sheds blood, else soon clan would rise against clan, tribe against tribe, and the wild, savage instincts of the people burst forth unchecked as in days not long past.

In the sacred groves by the Khond hamlets may still be seen the sacrificial

The Last Human Sacrifice

stakes to which human victims—boys, maidens, even old men and women, purchased or kidnapped from afar—were wont to be tied; and still is remembered the song of the sacrificing priest, in which he prayed for forgiveness as he slew the offering, sprinkled the blood on the fields, and divided the flesh among the assembled folk to plant in the earth so that the turmeric dye might grow red and the crops yield in abundance. Still in the Khond hamlets may be seen the bent-down old men and women once destined for the sacrifice, from which they were rescued by their English rulers.

Still yearly the officer in charge of the hill tracts travels through the hamlets, taking count of rescued victims, presenting each with prized strips of red cloth, a few leaves of tobacco, match-boxes or small mirrors, to induce them to come forward so that he may see that none of them is missing. He then calls on the village chiefs to renew the promise they swore in the past, that so long as the foreigner stands between them and the wrath of their gods no more human sacrifices will take place in the land, for years must elapse before the Khond will lay down his battle-axe and forget the lust of his Earth Goddess.

The simple people still dread the spirits who hover ever near—spirits of the earth, of the crops, of the flowing waters and moving winds; spirits of the rustling trees and solitary mountains; spirits who move amid the roar of the battle, and who planted the iron in the bowels of the earth wherewith man might shed his neighbour's blood. Yet to his gods, who live far and near, he builds no temples. Sometimes he plants by the roadside a rude stone image daubed red as a symbol of the former blood sacrifices.

Slowly and steadily as the forests are cleared and new roads open up the fertile valleys, temples filled with strange idols of Hindu gods are seen in the villages, the Khonds become fettered by the usages and customs of caste, the lowland priests gain power, and the primitive superstitions of the aboriginal folk are mingled with Aryan myths and legends till a new religious belief is formed, difficult to fathom, in which old and new, true and false, are so woven together by the subtle ingenuity of its founders, that it remains almost unassailable by the ever-continued attacks of civilisation and Christianity.

Were it not for these facts the Jesuit Father, the Abbé Leroux, who, not many years ago, took up his abode in the feverish tracts where the wild Khonds live, might have established his schools and drawn the people to listen to his message of peace and good will. When first he came among the Khonds he was wont to wander through their hamlets, watching the ways of the people, till soon his tall, erect form, clad in long white robe stretching down to his feet, and flowing white beard became familiar to the villagers, who ceased to view his visits with fear or to disappear into the jungle at his approach. Quickly he learned to speak all the dialects of the tribes, and it was said that he could converse with travellers from many parts of India in their own varied languages. Once when certain learned Brāhmans had travelled through the country on a pilgrimage to a famed temple in Central India, they told the villagers that the French *padre* had spoken to them in their own ancient Sanskrit language, arguing many points

The Last Human Sacrifice

of philosophy and doctrine known only to the deepest scholars in the land. Before many months had elapsed the gentle Jesuit Father's life of self-denial and his simple manners had so impressed the fierce Khonds of the hamlet of Adeva, that they readily granted him a piece of land near their village whereon to found a school and erect a chapel. There he patiently strove to teach, such of the Khonds and their children as he could assemble together, to read and write, each day's work commencing and ending with the singing of songs composed by the Abbé himself from the Christian Scriptures. By degrees, as his influence increased, he was able to build a home for some of the children of the wretched victims saved from the human sacrifice, who still led a lonely and degraded life on the land granted to them outside the Khond

and the Abbé Leroux

hamlets. Over this home he placed an aged matron, the wife of Billo the village weaver, hoping that in time, as the children grew up, taught and trained by himself, they would become helpers in the cause he had at heart—the regeneration of the Khonds.

Though the Abbé Leroux devoted his life to the work he had taken in hand he was no enthusiast, he knew that the course before him was long and tedious. He had weighed the minds of many peoples in many lands, and knew well the virtues and failings of the savages among whom he now lived. He never wearied when visiting the English officers of repeating the same note of warning, urging them never to rest assured that the custom of human sacrifice had died out from among the people. Watch, ever watch, were his constant words; old beliefs, old superstitions, die not in

The Last Human Sacrifice

a day nor in a generation. Though on the surface all may appear calm and fair as truth, still beneath lie buried the cankered roots ready to throw up a wide-spreading, noisome growth of foul wickedness and wrong.

The Abbé, who knew these things, however failed to take note of a low caste potter, by name Chengal, who had travelled up from the lowland plains, having been driven from his native village for the foul wrong he had done his neighbour's wife.

As the cunning hand of the potter deftly moulded the earth into strange shapes of water-pitchers and quaint idols, his mind noted how the simple drunken Khonds gathered round to watch the quick rolling twirl of his wheel and listen to his lying words. Though he had taken up his abode in the hamlet of Adeva, yet he was not allowed to live in the wide street where the low log huts of the Khonds were built, for the fierce folk scorn all who work with their hands and cannot plough the earth or wield the battle-axe. The potter had to live in one of the huts at the back of the village along with the weaver, the blacksmith, the village servants, and the seller of opium and arrack. When daily the jungle fever racked his bones, he learned to drink more than was good for him, as do all Khonds and lowland dwellers in the hills. In the long evenings, when he remained drinking in his hut, he was glad if Billo the weaver came in to sit with him, and talk of such things as the potter liked to listen to when foolish with the sweet fermented juice of the Mohwa flower.

"Abbā," cried the potter one night, as he and the weaver sat drinking together, "I was but an empty fool to

The Last Human Sacrifice

leave my wife and native village and come here to dwell in a wilderness. Do not our Shāstras tell us that a wise man should live only in a village where there is a temple, a Brāhman priest, and sweet water? The Khonds are cattle, and have no gods nor temples."

"Ah, you know nothing!" replied Billo, drawing a rolled-up leaf from his hair and proceeding to fill it with tobacco. "Who taught the Khonds to plough the earth and make terraces on the hillside to grow their rice? Was it not Tāri, the Earth Goddess? Have not I and my forefathers, the village weavers for generations past, brought the lovely boys and girls from the lowland villages to be offered as a sacrifice to the goddess in the sacred grove near the village. But now, since the red-faced foreigners rule the land, I get no wealth to buy offerings for the goddess, and live neglected at the back of the village with you and the blacksmith. Bah! the Khonds have become as monkeys who run through the forest, and as pigs who root up the ground. The goddess will yet tear them in pieces and blacken their homes if they listen not to her words, and give her the food she loves and sprinkle the blood on the fields."

"Godless husbands of one wife, they love blood and are as fierce as jungle cats," said the potter, raising a bottle with trembling hand and pouring the strong oily liquor into his open mouth, his lowland habits still clinging to him and preventing him touching the flask with his lips, "to-day I quaked as a reed shaken by the wind when the jabbering monkeys carried past one of their village to cut off his nose for looking at another man's wife."

"Bah!" cried Billo, pausing to help

The Last Human Sacrifice

himself from the potter's flask and drinking in the same manner as his companion. " What does a lowland potter know of the ways of a Khond ? If the fool's nose was cut some woman told her husband to do it so that the village might think she had a lover. The women do as they like, and often marry two husbands. If a woman sits with her lover in the forest or in her home, she need but place her lover's shoes or bow and arrow across the path or on the threshold and the husband dare not pass. Why not? The women stay at home and tend the cattle while the men lie drunk under the sago-trees. Oh ! the Khond women know their value, and will run away if not obeyed. How can a Khond get a new wife ? He must go to a far-off village and pay the purchase money, or else serve for six months in the home of her parents, and even then he must carry her off from her relatives by force. Ho! ho!" laughed Billo, noticing the eager looks with which the potter, as he leaned forward, listened to his words, "Ho! ho! to think of Chengal the potter running off with a Khond woman and laying his earthen pot across the path to prevent her husband following. Why, the village bachelors would place it on your head, tie you to your potter's wheel, and hack you to pieces as it whirled round, while the husband and wife would stand by laughing. Last year," continued the weaver, sinking his voice, "when the English sahib cut down one of their sago-palms to make a salad of the young, tender leaves, they tied lighted tow to an arrow, and shot it into the thatched roof of the house where he dwelt. No Khond would then re-thatch the roof, and the sahib had to sleep under the trees in the forest."

"What becomes of the unmarried girls in the eventime? I see none of them in the hamlet," asked the potter, not heeding the words of the weaver.

"Ah! you have not found out, though you have lived here six months," replied Billo, smiling. "You know the big log hut at the end of the village, there at sunset they lock up all the unmarried girls and place the key in charge of an old woman. In a similar house at the other end of the village they lock up the bachelors. If they find you prowling about the hamlet in the eventime, they will lock you up with the bachelors."

"One might as well be a croaking frog at the bottom of a dried-up well as live here alone," cried Chengal in angry tones. "If I am not to have a wife like all other respectable men, I will leave the village. Why cannot I as well as a monkey Khond buy a wife?"

"Women are few in the Khond villages," replied the weaver, quietly, watching the potter; "the Khonds kill their female children, and keep but a few. A wife is dear to buy. Besides, you are old and ugly."

"Ah!" answered the potter, growing cautious, and not noticing the taunt, "the Khond women are flat-nosed, half-clad, black witches. A man is perhaps better alone."

"I know a maiden of your own caste, who has not yet seen fifteen crops," said the weaver, gazing through the thick smoke at the black thatched roof in an absent manner, pretending not to notice the eager looks of the potter who, half drunk, bent forward to catch every word.

"Her people owe me yet for the cloth

The Last Human Sacrifice

I weaved for her last year. She will soon get a husband, and then they will pay me. Fifty rupees they hope to get. Yesterday her parents asked me if I would travel to the low country and find her a husband. Ah!" continued Billo, pausing to light his tobacco, and watching the face of the potter from under his half-closed eyes, "ah! the lovely-eyed Kāmākshi walks like a drunken elephant. I could swear on a tiger-skin that she paints her eyes black."

"Vile weaver of coarse cloths," interrupted Chengal, "what mean you by saying that a woman of my caste lives in the jungle, among people who have no caste? Know you not that a Brāhman will sleep in the house of a man of my caste?"

"I know you and your caste, you drunken moulder of pots," answered Billo, unmoved; "many of your people

and the Abbé Leroux

when in want have sold to me and my fathers their children. Kāmākshi is no black-skinned Khond woman. Her cheeks are like the ripe mango fruit. May I fall to dust like that of the ant-hill if her hair is not black as charred wood and long as the trail of the serpent. May I become leprous as the lizard if her ears are not as big as lotus leaves."

"Wretched bearer of other men's messages, you lie like a ploughing Brāhman of Orissa, if you say that a woman of my caste lives in the hamlet and I know it not."

Billo answered not, but sunk his head on his breast as if half asleep.

"Billo," continued the potter, fearing he had offended his companion, "I have heard that you can weave cloths fringed with silk and gold thread if you are well paid. The people say that as you have no male child, and your wife is growing old, you intend to seek a new wife. Billo, I am a poor potter; how can I gather up wealth to buy your cloths and help you to purchase a new wife; but I know my people would send me twenty rupees if they heard I was seeking Kāmākshi? Tell me, friend of the Khonds, how came a woman of my caste to the hamlet?"

The weaver looked long at the wizened face and cunning eyes of the potter before he replied, "Chengal, moulder of clay, I will tell you, though no one else in the hamlet knows the story, and little good will it do you.

"Some forty years ago, I was sent to the plains to purchase or kidnap victims, thirty or more. In those days, Tāri the goddess was raging through the land, she had swept away the rains and sent the tigers down

and the Abbé Leroux

from the mountain tops, so that the people were afraid to leave their homes. Among those I brought back were a boy and girl of your caste. They were not sacrificed, for the English sahib released them. So they married and settled in our hamlet, and Kāmākshi was born to them. Eh! why do you sleep, fool of a potter? I alone know now where Kāmākshi is, and without my aid you cannot get her. I bought her father and mother, and the man who marries their daughter pays me fifty rupees. By the claws of the tiger it is not much; half will have to go to her parents."

"Fifty rupees," repeated Chengal, with drunken gravity, "fifty rupees, fifty cowries you mean, base-born seller of another man's children; why in my village I could buy ten girls of my caste for fifty rupees."

The Last Human Sacrifice

"So have I, friend Chengal, but we live in the hills, and women are scarce. What women of your caste would come here to die of fever? Fifty rupees, oh! oh! frog at the bottom of a dried-up well."

Long Chengal and Billo watched each other's eyes through the thick smoke with which the room was filled. At length the potter rose, and with uncertain steps made his way to the corner of the room, and there unlocking a wooden box carried back to the weaver a heavy bag of rupees. Seizing the weaver's outstretched hand, he whispered in his ear, still holding the bag—

"Brother-in-law, fifty long-saved rupees, all I own in the world. Will Kāmākshi's mother bring her here in the morning?"

"Ha! ha!" laughed the weaver, "you will have to visit the maiden yourself. Bring her a rich cloth and some jewels, if she consent not, then her mother——"

A significant look passed between the potter and the weaver, and as the latter seized the bag and tied it beneath his waistcloth he turned to leave. Before, however, he reached the door, the potter seized him hastily by the arm and whispered hoarsely—

"You have not yet said where I am to find my loved wife, the bright-eyed Kāmākshi."

Billo stood for a moment by the door looking into the black darkness, and then turned and whispered in the ear of his companion.

"Kāmākshi lives under the charge of my wife, to whom I will speak, in the home built near the village by the French padre, the Abbé Leroux."

II.

NEXT morning Billo, the weaver, sat on the verandah of his house at the end of the hamlet, waiting for his wife to come from the school of the French padre and prepare his mid-day meal. As he watched her shamble along down the middle of the street as fast as her aged limbs would carry her, he noticed that her head shook and her lips moved quickly as though she were muttering to herself. When she approached nearer and saw the angry looks of her husband, her thin, bent-down body seemed to shrink more than ever, while her shaking hand hastily drew her scanty raiment, which reached but half way down to her knee, closer round her shrivelled, ash-coloured shoulder. Silently and with bent-down eyes she stole towards the verandah and, seating herself near the door of the house a few paces behind her husband, commenced once more to moan and wring her hands. She heeded not as Billo glared at her out of the corner of his eyes with growing wrath, but continued muttering to herself—

"Three children have I born, all useless girls; never once has a boy been born to us; never once has a full crop grown in our fields since the time the Earth Goddess last received a sacrifice. Ten girls, all sacred to the mother, live in the school kept by the French padre, and none of our village has the heart of a tiger to give the mother the food she loves. One, only one, the mother longs for; then my husband would gain wealth and buy a young wife to fetch water from the river and cook his food, to bear him a boy child to continue our race. He is an owl that sits on the housetop bringing ruin to the family."

"Where am I to get money to buy a girl?" cried the weaver, now roused to anger by her taunts. "Toothless tigress, fed by the food of another, get more money from your master, the French padre, and I will bring home a girl for you to beat."

"The padre will give us no more money," she fiercely answered, raising her thin arm and shaking it at her husband in rage. "To-day he drove me out of the school, and told me to come no more. May the mother turn him into a tiger to devour the girls he keeps from her."

"Mother of girls," cried the weaver, "your words are as the cawing of a crow. If you bring not home the padre's money, I will tie you to a tree as food for jackals."

"Unmarried man, you rave as the madman in the village whom the people keep locked up in his house, chained to a log of wood. You and your low-caste maker of pots have taken the food from our stomachs. When he spoke to the foul fiend, Kāmākshi, the padre came and beat him across the back with a heavy stick. The girl, who took the potter's rupees and jewels, laughed as she heard him cry out, and clapped her hands when the padre drove us forth from the school."

"Listen to my words, dried-up mother of girls," said the weaver, scowling fiercely from beneath his shaggy brows at his wife, who sat trembling with mingled fear and anger. "You remember how, five years ago, I told the

Khonds that you stole out in the dead of night and roamed through the village in the form of a tigress. They then made you eat blows, and have ever since prevented you from coming near the village, except in the daytime to cook my food. If you tell of what you have seen to-day, I will swear before the Khonds that I have seen you assume the form of a tigress during the daytime, and then they will pull out your teeth and slay you as a witch. Go now to the padre, fall at his feet, and tell him that the potter brought Kāmākshi a message of love from a Khond of another tribe in a far-off village. Tell the girl that the potter will give her rich jewels and rupees if she makes the long-bearded foreigner believe your words, else we will slay her parents in the sacred grove. Go, the anger of the foreigner will have passed like a

and the Abbé Leroux

hot-day cloud; he knows not the way of our people, and how when we smile we love to throw dust in his eyes."

So saying, the weaver hurried out; but as he approached the potter's house he grew uneasy, for the door was closed, and in front, beneath the open thatched shed, the earth lay dry on the wheel. Hastily throwing open the door, he looked into the dimly lighted room, where, in a corner, he discerned the potter lying half asleep on a cot.

On seeing the weaver, he raised himself and, shaking his hand in anger, burst into a loud torrent of abuse.

"May you and all your race be suspended by a rope, which is ever gnawed by rats, over the bottomless pit. Who am I to be beaten like a pariah dog with a stick by a drunken priest of a godless temple? May the goddess of small-pox ride on an ass through your villages and the goddess of cholera slay your sons. I, Chengal, the potter, in whose house a Brāhman priest has eaten food, driven through the streets as if I were a base-born son of a dancing girl. To the maiden have I given the nose-rings of my wife and ten rupees, yet she laughed in my face when the long-bearded padre beat me like a dog."

"Bah," said the weaver, leaning against the doorpost, "you can laugh in the beard of the French priest when you bring Kāmākshi to your home. Spoke I not truth when I told you she was fair as a girl of the lowland villages?"

"Listen, blinking owl of ill omen," cried Chengal, fiercely, "half of the fifty rupees you can keep if you help me to drive the French padre from the village, and as for Kāmākshi, who stole my money and jewels and laughed in my face, you can keep her for yourself."

Billo stood thinking as he watched the potter, who had risen, and now paced up and down the room muttering angry words to himself.

"Chengal," at length he said, "you speak like the wind, knowing not the ways of our people. When I seek a wife I seek one from a distant tribe, as do the Khonds. Besides, I have paid the parents of Kāmākshi the purchase money in full, and they have consented to give you the girl. How, then, can we take her back? Is she not yours?"

"Do as you will with the girl," replied Chengal, in fierce anger. "I have sworn by the black Kāli that she and the French padre will yet eat dirt. I took count of each blow, and all will be paid back with interest. Let him

The Last Human Sacrifice

watch the food he eats and the milk he drinks. I have sworn to build a temple to Kāli in the village when he dies. Come, now, weaver, in the forest I will show the black Khonds how we honour our goddess Kāli, for never yet has a new temple been erected in her honour but we shed the blood of a human victim before her image."

"Brother," said Billo, starting, "you lie like a lowland trader. I have travelled in your villages and never yet seen aught but the blood of goats shed before the mother Kāli. It is the Goddess of the Earth, the loved Tāri, alone who demands human blood."

"Bah," interrupted Chengal, "wise man in your own house and a fool in the streets, you know not the mysteries of our temples. Once we appease the mother Kāli with a human offering, ever afterwards she is satisfied with the blood of goats and fowls. Now, beloved of the gods and knower of nothing, will you swear that the Khonds never offer a sacrifice in the sacred grove to their mother Tāri?"

Billo, the weaver, looked warily out of the house and round the room to see that no one was near, and then beckoning him to his side, whispered—

"Once in twelve years a sacrifice takes place among one or other of the tribes who worship Tāri. Last year the word was sent to our hamlet that this year our turn would come to provide a victim, but we fear the English rulers, and have none ready for the sacrifice. The offering must be given by the parents or purchased for a price, for the Khonds like not the guilt to fall on their own heads. The Khond but obeys the goddess, and gives her her own. Who now is to give a victim to

The Last Human Sacrifice

Tāri? The Khonds have given me the money to purchase one, but I fear to go to the lowland plains, for the rulers have sworn to hang me if I am found in the villages."

"Then go," cried Chengal, with flashing eyes, his thin arm raised above his head exultingly, "go quick, send out word to the Khonds of the tribes who honour the goddess. Bid them assemble here with the heads of the villages and chiefs of their clans, for the offering is now ready. Let the Khonds pay me back the money I gave you for Kāmākshi and she will be theirs. No blame will rest on their heads, for it is I and her parents who give her as a sacrifice. Speed the word from village to village, but let each Khond who hears the message swear on the earth, on the tiger skin, on the anthill, to hold the secret in silence, for

and the Abbé Leroux

if the English officer or French padre hear, the villages will be burned to the ground, the sacred groves will be cut down, and all of us carried off to the lowland plains, where we will surely be hung. Let the message go quick, for even now the fierce Kāli knows our thoughts and has entered into my veins. Wealth according to their desire belongs to those who serve her. She whispers in the ear of her lord and husband, the three-eyed Siva, to forgive the past and future sins of those who wait in her temples. Holy mother Kāli, thy worship will yet take the place of Tāri in the Khond villages, the people will bring thee the food thou lovest, and ever after present goats and fowls to thy dread image. Appoint me, O mother, thy priest. The sacred grove will echo with the cries of thy worshippers; the white walls of thy temple will shine

The Last Human Sacrifice

beneath the tamarind-trees. Hasten, O mother, drive the foreign priest from the land, raze his schools and chapel to the ground, cover them with ashes, and the Khonds will dance with wild joy as they slay the victim till the earth shakes beneath their feet, even as it did when thou didst dance on the bodies of thy fallen foes. Abide in the village. I, thy priest, will present the offerings of the people before thine image.

"Go now, weaver of cloths, you will yet grow rich with the offerings of the people when the loved image of Kāli takes the place of the red-smeared stone, the symbol of Tāri. Go, make all ready, for the sacrifice will take place on the tenth day from now. I will build a temple of stone and earth, and place therein an image of Kāli, marked with blood, so that the Khonds may imagine that it is their loved goddess, Tāri."

and the Abbé Leroux

Excited by the words of the potter, Billo, the weaver, hastened back to the hamlet and sent out word to the fields and forests, telling the Khonds and their headmen to assemble that night to hear a message that had been sent from the people of their tribe, respecting the sacrifice to the Earth Goddess. He then made his way to the hut of the Soondi, whose business it was to distil the sap of the sago-palm and juice of the fallen flowers of the mohwa-trees, and told him to bring forth as many pots of strong drink as he possessed, or could make ready, for great would be the rejoicing in the village when the Khonds assembled together to listen to the message from the goddess.

The sun had long sunk below the forest-clad hill-tops surrounding the valley in which lay the hamlet of Adeva, before the Khonds, already half-

The Last Human Sacrifice

intoxicated, uttering fierce cries, brandishing their battle-axes, or aimlessly discharging their arrows into the surrounding darkness, commenced to assemble together, some dancing beneath the massive cotton-trees in the centre of the village; others engaging here and there in mock combat near the huge log-fires, which burned brightly in front of each house. Soon the scene became wilder as the Khonds gathered in from the fields and surrounding hamlets, or hurried down from the mountain-sides, where for days past they had been busy clearing the fertile soil for cultivation, ringing the tall forest trees, burning the high jungle grass and dried undergrowth, so that now a broad belt of fire, halfway up the surrounding hills, enclosed the valley. Above, the heavens shone white with bands of deep clustering stars; below, in the hamlet, it seemed

and the Abbé Leroux

as if demons and foul spirits danced amid the flare and smoke of the torches the Khonds carried in their hands. As their eyes grew red and their throats parched, the Soondi was ready with his maddening drink to rouse still further their wild passions.

At a signal from the headman of the hamlet, the Khonds, some wearing buffalo horns tied to their foreheads, others, with their hair wound round in a circle on one side of their heads, gaudily decorated with strips of red cloth and brilliant peacock's or jungle fowl's feathers, ranged themselves in a circle close together, their elbows pressed to their sides, and commenced their wild, mad, tribal dance. With bodies bent down, eyes fixed on the ground, each dancer raised his feet in high regular step, all keeping pace, till by degrees the circle moved round quicker and

The Last Human Sacrifice

quicker, no word being uttered, save when now and then a wild, muffled cry arose, proclaiming the fierce excitement of one or other of the dancers.

The potter and the weaver stood aloof with the headman watching the dance, and waiting for the time to come when the Khonds would be ready to listen to their words.

Suddenly the wife of the weaver rushed forth from the darkness, breaking the ring, and taking her place between two young Khonds commenced to dance, step by step, with the others, she, the only woman present. Her feet were raised high; her shrieks burst forth wildly, as bent down she danced on as if possessed by an evil spirit; her scanty cloth leaving uncovered her withered breasts; her coarse grey hair standing out round her head and shoulders in wild confusion; her face daubed with saffron, looking weird and fierce in the bright glare from the burning torches and log fires piled up high by the women and children with huge logs of wood.

Wilder grew the dance, till one fierce shriek arose as the wife of the weaver rushed forward towards the centre of the ring, foaming at the mouth, convulsively writhing her frail body as moaning she fell to the ground. With frantic yells the dancers crowded round, each savagely fighting to get near and hear the words that fell from the lips of the woman now supposed to be seized by the spirit of the goddess. Loud came the cries from the struggling crowd—

" The goddess has entered into the wife of the weaver, let her now declare to us Her will. Did not the goddess teach the wife of the weaver to assume the form of a tigress in the night-time ?

The Last Human Sacrifice

Now the words of the goddess hang on her lips; let her speak, and we listen. Who are we to be swept from the land like ploughed earth down the mountainside by the heavy rain? Our fields are lying waste; the samber deer eat our crops, and the wild forest pig root up the earth; too long have we neglected the Earth Goddess, Tāri. Let her now speak, and we will do her will."

As the weaver's wife struggled on the ground, those nearest listened to the words that were shrieked from her foaming lips, and cried them to the others, till the air rang with the supposed commands of the Goddess of the Earth.

"Tāri calls. She waits in the sacred grove.

"Last year the tiger she sent slew the village priest. The goddess will yet send tigers, so that the fields will be deserted, and the mountain paths grow covered with jungle as the people sit at home afraid to go out. The goddess cries for a sacrifice. The turmeric will grow red, and the crops plentiful, when the blood is sprinkled and the flesh planted in the earth. No blame will rest on the Khonds, the blame will rest on the goddess who demands the sacrifice, and on those who sell their children. For twelve years no sacrifice has taken place in the sacred grove. Let the people swear on the earth to obey the goddess. Let them swear not to tell the French priest, or send word to the English rulers."

At these words a murmur arose among the crowd, and there was an angry silence, till a young Khond, whose battle-axe, with three bands of silver round its long handle, had a blade divided into nine broad teeth, and whose hair was decorated with brighter cloth and longer feathers than that of the others, stepped forward, and first saluting the headman with folded hands raised to his head, the thumbs touching his nose, turned towards the Khonds, and spoke in slow, clear voice—

"Let the Khonds hear my words, then let the headman speak wisdom. Am I not known to the Khonds? Have I not slain a tiger with the iron-shod end of a bamboo pole, and did not the English sahib give me a gun as a reward? Since that day have I done any work; do not the Khonds honour me as having the heart of a tiger; may I not go into any man's house and take all I desire? Let them now listen. The Khonds lie not like the lowland dwellers in the plains; they are one race bound together, not divided into caste. Yet in our villages live foreigners, base-

and the Abbé Leroux

born men, who plough not nor fight, but work with their hands. Base-born slaves, who live not in the Khond street, whom we, kings of the hills, found here dwelling as pigs when we came from our ancient home; they lie and steal like lowland thieves. Let us then all swear on the earth to do the bidding of the goddess, and slay with lingering torture the man, woman, or child, who bears news to the foreign priest or hill police."

As the Khond ceased, and stepped back amid shouts of applause and approval, the weaver came forward, and throwing himself prone on the ground in front of the headman, waited for permission to speak, which being granted, he rose, and facing the Khonds, spoke with a loud voice, as one accustomed to be listened to:—" Khonds of Adeva, I, Billo, the village Dombo, bearer of your messages, and buyer of your offerings, will take the oath. But where is the victim? Fifty rupees has the headman given me to purchase for the sacrifice, but have not our rulers told us that they will hang me if I go through the villages in search of a new victim?"

A roar of discontent rose from amid the Khonds as with drunken recklessness they flourished their battle-axes, and, twirling them round, hurled them in the air, around and above the head of the weaver, who stood unmoved, watching the scene, as one well accustomed to the wild ways of the people. In an instant the wife of the weaver struggled out of the arms of two of the village matrons who were leading her away and, rushing back, cried in wild excitement—

"Let not the words of the goddess be disobeyed, else ruin, disease and pestilence will prowl through your homes. Let the stranger in our midst provide the victim, and then no blame will rest on us. Call forth the potter and let the Khonds pay him the price he gave for the maiden he has bought from her parents, and let him go seek a wife for himself among his own people."

"The voice of the goddess speaks in her words," cried the weaver. "The parents of Kāmākshi sold her to the potter; let him go seek a wife in the lowland villages, and let the Khonds bid me pay him the fifty rupees he gave for the girl. Let the parents of Kāmākshi be brought here to say if they have sold their daughter to the potter for fifty rupees."

Quickly the parents of Kāmākshi were fetched from the hut where they lived outside the village limit, for they never joined in the Khond life, but lived poor and neglected on the land given them, when they had been rescued from

The Last Human Sacrifice

the sacrifice for which they had in past days been purchased by the weaver, who alone knew their race and parentage. Trembling the old man and woman told how their daughter Kāmākshi had been taken from their home by the French priest, and how they were glad to receive the rupees of the potter to whom they had given her, and that they now wished not to see her again. As the Khonds heard the words they crowded round the parents of Kāmākshi, crying out that their reward would be as great as if they themselves had been sacrificed in their youth to the goddess who would ever in the future hold them under her protection.

Loud cries arose as the headman raised his hand and stood waiting to speak; his short, thin beard, piercing eyes and keen glance, broad nose, firm forehead, full chest, thin waist, and high, arched instep marking him out as a Khond of the Khonds, one who knew no fear of man, but whose simple mind dreaded the unknown forces that lay hid all around him in the dim mysteries of nature. Quietly the Khonds squatted round to listen in silence to the words of their chief. Twice as he strove to speak the words died away in his throat, and as he bowed his head on his breast, women's tears trickled down the cheeks of the fierce clansmen who had oft witnessed the feats of daring, and knew the cunning skill of their loved chief. At length his sentences came slow, till, as he continued, the wild, fierce words came flowing from his lips, and his form grew erect and defiant, as each sentence was followed by loud cries of approval from his listening people.

"Khonds of Adeva, have not I and my forefathers oft led you to battle?

The Last Human Sacrifice

Two years ago we slew sixty men of the clan who sacrifice not to Tāri. When the arrows fell as hail and the stones came from the slings like rain, was not I the first to hew the hand from one of our vaunting foes and hang it on the tree as an offering to the God of Battle? How many times have you carried me home covered with wounds? Khonds of Adeva, far away lies the place of judgment for those of our race who die. The way is dreary, the river flows swift round the smooth mountain side, where the God of Judgment sits waiting for our spirits. All of my forefathers have leaped the flowing river and found firm foothold on the slippery rocks, for the goddess whom they served held their footsteps firm and led them safe to the summit of the mountain to receive their reward from the God of Judgment. Not one of them has fallen

and the Abbé Leroux

down the steep ascent, and returned to the land of the living deformed in body or limb. We have all lived among you fair, strong men. We have led you to battle, joined in your dances, chased the tiger to its lair, driven the bear and cheetah from their caves in the hills. We have chosen your priests and made peace with the English soldiers when we saw they were many and had guns and swords against which our battle-axes, bows and arrows could not fight. Have we ever lied or spoken words of folly? Let the English sahibs keep their rescued victims from the goddess. We can buy new ones. The goddess calls. The summons has come from the clans. For twelve years the earth has cried in our hamlet with hunger, for no sacrifice has taken place in the sacred grove. You have heard her words, will you face her wrath if dis-

The Last Human Sacrifice

obeyed? See, the fire creeps up the mountain side, the earth lies bare, will it yield if the flesh be not planted and the blood sprinkled? Swear, then, on the earth to keep secret the rites we will perform, and all the clans who share in the sacrifice will call the Khonds in the hamlet of Adeva men with the hearts of tigers. By the hillside and by the mountain paths you have placed stones and daubed them with red, to keep in your memories the blood sacrifice. Let, now, the priest take the symbol, and set it as he will in the sacred grove, that the goddess may know we have not forgotten her. In the villages of the plains, in the chief hamlets in the hills, the people now build temples and set therein the symbols of the spirits they appease with the blood of fowls and goats. Listen, now, to my words. Our priest has been slain by a tiger sent by the angry goddess. In his place I appoint Chengal, the potter, as priest, to carry out the sacred rites, and on my head be the blame if any part of the rites be not fully carried out ten days from now. Let Chengal be the priest, and let the blame of the bloodshed be on his head, for he has sold us the victim, the maiden Kāmākshi."

For ten days the Khonds held revel ; for ten days the potter laboured in the sacred grove, building a temple ten feet square, with pointed roof, wherein he placed the image of Kāli, a fierce image of the goddess, with red streaked face and lolling tongue, and four arms, one hand bearing a sword, one hand holding a human head, dripping blood, one hand pointing to the heavens, one hand held forth to her worshippers ; her eyes painted black with white circles, her

The Last Human Sacrifice

girdle painted with dead men's hands, her necklace painted with dead men's skulls.

On the third day before the sacrifice the Abbé Leroux was told by the wife of the weaver that Kāmākshi had fled from the home during the night, to seek a Khond whom she loved in a far-off hamlet, and that the rest of his girls had fled to their parents, fearing his anger.

That night Kāmākshi, stupefied with opium, lay in the house of the potter, and so she remained for three days, being led out during the eventime to the sacred grove, where she was honoured and worshipped, for the Khonds hold the victim sacred even before the sacrifice takes place.

Before sunrise of the fourth day there was not a Khond hamlet within sixty miles of the grove in which the sacred

DAHA THE POTTER CLANGED HIS CYMBALS.

flesh had not been planted, for swift runners quickly bore their share from post to post along the lonely mountain paths.

Ever afterwards the Khonds of Adeva worshipped the goddess Kāli, bringing the flesh of sheep and goats to be eaten by the weaver and the potter, and no more was the worship of Tāri heard of in the hamlet. For long the Abbé Leroux went in vain through the neighbouring villages seeking out children for his school, and daily Chengal the potter clanged his cymbals in fierce exultation as he thought of the downcast face of the Jesuit Father who never knew how the shrine of the lowland goddess Kāli had risen in the Khond hamlet of Adeva.

THE DREAM OF LIFE.

"You see the concordance of Indian, Greek, and German metaphysics; the world is Māyā, is illusion," says Cankara. "It is a world of shadows, not of realities," says Plato. "It is appearance only, not the thing in itself," says Kant.—DEUSSEN, "Philosophy of the Vedānta," p. 332.

THE DREAM OF LIFE.

I.

"Have you no thought, O Dreamer, that it may be all Maya, illusion."—WALT WHITMAN.

ALL Hindu people bow down before the Brāhmans, counting them as holy, of divine birth, very gods among men. Inheritors and guardians of the sacred lore and learning of the past, the Brāhmans trace back their descent from the ancient Vedic sages, and claim kindred with the Aryan races of the West. Tall and well formed, with high foreheads, thin, compressed nostrils, and of fair complexion, they look down with haughty contempt on the dark-skinned descendants of the aboriginal inhabitants of the land, holding themselves aloof from all, allowing no low-caste villager even to pass down the streets where their rich houses are built. Asserting that in the beginning they were created from the head of the Creator, that all other castes—soldiers, merchants, and servile people — were produced from the arms, body, or feet of God for the sole protection of their will and power, they have so moulded the laws, religions, and customs of the people that the duty of every man in life, from birth to the funeral pyre, is clearly laid down, and none dares depart from the course thus allotted. As counsellors of kings, as scholars, poets, and philosophers, as priests in the temples, and writers in the offices of

of Life &

their rulers, wherever they may be found, they have made their learning honoured and their power feared.

To-day, wise men in our own land find in the depths of their philosophy all that has been reasoned out by the ancient philosophers of Greece and the deepest minds of to-day in the West. Others, vainly seeking to pierce through the dark mystery of Creation, would fain believe that to the ascetic Brāhman sages and Mahātmas of India, secret knowledge of the Unknown has been revealed, and that their souls, rising above all the trammels of the body, wander free at will.

Renowned above all the Brāhmans of India for his learning in the Vedas, Upanishads, and Vedānta, was the holy and self-subdued Satyakāma, the Lover of Truth. For many generations past his forefathers had lived wealthy and honoured in the well-known village of Achinta, in the south where the Brāhman is still held holy as of old. Step by step he had followed out all the rules and ordinances laid down of old for the guidance for his high order. Sitting at the feet of his Guru, a learned teacher, he had passed from youth to manhood, learning by rote the entire Sanskrit scriptures, glosses, and commentaries. In manhood, self-contained and subdued, he had poured forth to scholars, seeking knowledge, the stored treasures of his mind, his subtle brain piercing deep through the hidden meaning of the ancient sayings of the Vedic sages. All debts to the gods and forefathers he had paid. The temple priests had gained rich presents from his hands when they performed the religious rites for his ancestors and family; none of his caste had ever been known to depart

of Life

from his home empty-handed. When his wife died he mourned for many months, knowing that his life had been rent in twain, and that nevermore would the depths of his heart be read through and through. Though three sons and three fair daughters lived to hand down his race unsullied to future generations, yet he bowed his head before the words of his people and knowing the disgrace that clung to an unmarried man of his caste, had taken to his home a second wife, the youthful Sītā, daughter of his kinsman.

At length, having lived to see children of his children and his own grey hairs he longed to be finally freed from all desires of the body, and end his days as a hermit in the depths of the forest, far away from the abode of man, brooding over the mystery of that secret, breathed forth in the infinite past, still

The Dream

ever echoing back to his soul weird whispers from the endless bounds of space.

The day when, according to the customs of his forefathers, the ascetic sage journeyed forth from his native village, accompanied only by his gentle wife Sītā, was one long after remembered by the grave elders, and ever held sacred by the village maidens of Achinta. Early, when the gleam of the morning sun shone softly on the red-tiled houses in the wide Brāhman street, groups of sedate holy men gathered together beneath the shade of the sacred banyan trees, waiting in silence, before the abode of Satyakāma, to accompany him on his way as far as the village limits. Close at hand, beneath the deep shadows of the high pinnacles of the temple, bright-eyed dancing girls stood ready to strew rice and sweet-scented flowers before the path of the youthful Sītā, loved throughout the village for her beauty and piety. When at length Satyakāma came forth from his home his stern features moved not as the holy men pressed forward to bow down before him in reverend salutation while the dancing girls drew near singing hymns of praise to their gods. He had long since rooted out from his heart all the fond delusions of life. He but now hoped to reach the lonely solitudes of the forest, commune with his own soul, seeking that haven of rest where the result of his good and evil actions would never more throb down through the ages producing birth and rebirth after their own kind.

With white robes wrapped round his folded arms he strode down the wide Brāhman street, where the lazy, sad-eyed oxen lay half asleep beneath the thick shade of the holy fig-trees, and the naked children stood gazing in wonder, with wide open black eyes, at the passing crowd, or sat by the wayside raising mud heaps, crowned with yellow flowers, to bow down before them with folded hands, imitating in sad fancy the manner of their parents. Slowly he passed on through the busy streets of the merchants, where in the heat and thick red dust the ponderous bulls, sacred to Siva, broke their rough way through the crowd surging to and fro round the deep verandahs heavily laden with baskets of grain or filled with strange idols cunningly worked in the sandal wood of Tripati and roughly hewn brass of Benares. Reaching the outskirts of the village he hastened on past the palm leaf round huts of the outcast pariahs who, dreading lest even their shadows might fall before the path of those born

of Life &

from the head of the Creator, lay prone on the ground in the midst of mire where wallowed unclean pigs. He stayed not to gaze where the trunks of the dark green mango-trees were painted in fantastic bands of red and white to ward off the evil eye of the passer-by from the heavy fruit that clustered overhead. Wrapt in deep thought he journeyed on beneath the shaded groves of the stately cocoanut-trees whose broad leaves rustled in the morning wind, on between the thick edges of the screw pines, where the golden chrysallises of butterflies glistened on the edges of the spiked trailing leaves, and venomous snakes lay hid amid the thick twisted roots, till at length he reached the village tank in the midst of the rich rice-fields. There he stayed to once more gather up the sacred waters in his hands and scatter them for the last time

The Dream

to the four quarters as he muttered prayers to the gods and fathers.

The sun had risen high in the heavens ere he reached the running waters of the wide river forming the village boundary, where he parted from the following twice-born caste men, while Sītā took her last sad farewell of the fond companions of her youth, who bowed down to touch her raiment, their soft limbs gleaming olive-coloured through their white robes yet wet with the waters of the sacred tank. So, followed by his wife, even as Rāma was followed by his Sītā in days of old when faith was firm and men and women holy and pure, the ascetic sage left his home to travel for many months towards the far north. Long they journeyed together, through the sacred portals of holy Tripati, across the broad Godaveri, over the burning sands of the Kistna, towards the lofty

of Life ❧

peaks of Mahendragiri, till they reached the heights of Kailāsa where they took up their lonely abode, tended by the wild hill people who lived in the surrounding forests. There for many weary months, Satyakāma sitting in strange postures, deeply pondered over the teaching of the ancient Vedic sages, performed all the penances and fastings, suppression of the breath, ordained from of old for all those who would free their souls from the defilement of the body and pierce through the secret of life and death, birth and rebirth.

From the precipitous peaks of the lofty mountain he gazed towards the distant plains and thought how, in the villages, dotted here and there along the silvery lines of the broad rivers, amid the busy haunts of men, the labourer ever toiled for leave to live, how the rich feverishly struggled through thank-

The Dream

less days and sleepless nights to increase the wealth they hoarded, how the poet and pandit hungered for fame, and the lover sighed for love, all wearily knowing deep down in their hearts that their desire was a bubble destined to disappear when grasped. He looked away towards the stretching sand of the far off sea shore, where the rolling waters lapped in long white lines by the side of the green snake and sleeping turtle basking in the sunshine; he looked across the unrippled surface of the dark blue ocean as it lay speckled with the faint shadows of the light azure cloud flecks floating gently over the face of the deep heavens, and saw how beyond was still the mystery of endless space over which the unconscious soul of the universe breathed calm from before all time, one only without a second.

His soul then rested in peace while

of Life &

he pondered over the sad secret, ever held dear by all holy men of his race, that our life is but an uneasy dream, conjuring forth diversity soon to vanish away when all passes into unconscious rest to evermore sleep in unison. Long he meditated in deep thought over the treasured lore of his land, telling how the life that throbbed in the burning rays of the sun, in the cold gleam of the moon, in the deep love of his wife, within himself and all creation, was the unreal fancy of a dream conjured up by the deluding power of Māyā, which in the beginning woke up the universe from unconscious rest, to dream the sad dream of life soon to cease when the soul awakes seeing unity in all. By some in his land the One God might be seen as real in the wilderness, by some in the rushing waters, by some in the images they fashioned and worshipped,

The Dream

he alone longed to find a safe release from endless transmigration of his soul through birth after rebirth, ever producing desire, sorrow, and loss. He longed that his soul might pass into unconscious rest, equal and one with Brahma, pure existence, thought, and joy, with naught second over which it would ever rejoice or be sad, never more to be awakened to dream again the sad Dream of Life.

II.

"We are no other than a moving row
  Of magic shadow-shapes that come and go.

  .   .   .   .   .

Impotent pieces of the game he plays
Upon the chequer-board of nights and days."
OMAR KHAYYĀM.

WHILE Satyakāma dreamed on the mountain summit an English traveller, having heard of the strange hermit of Mount Kailāsa, resolved to climb the steep ascent and see face to face the ascetic sage who, unmoved by the rise and fall of empires, still stood firm and fixed in his own faith and belief. For days he journeyed from the lowland plains, toiling up the mountain

The Dream

sides, towards the far off peaks. There, beneath the deep shades of the forest, where creepers, rich with flowers, stretched from branch to branch of the massive teak-trees, growing around in virgin luxuriance, all lay wrapped in silence, save when the ripple of the silvery streams broke the deep stillness, or the pitiful plaint of the peewit rose sad. At times the sudden shriek of the peacock, warning the timid deer of the stealthy approach of the tiger, made the heart of the traveller stand still, astounded at the deep solitudes into which he had penetrated. Ascending higher up the mountain-paths he now and then paused to watch the plains beneath, where the peaceful villages shone in the midst of the rice-fields, growing green beneath the rays of the burning sun.

At length, one evening, as the cold

of Life ❧

grey mist was fast creeping up the precipitous ravines on the mountain side, he reached the summit of the far-famed Kailāsa, where, half concealed beneath the forest trees, he saw the leaf-thatched hut of the ascetic sage. On the edge of the mountain stood Satyakāma, gazing with deep-sunk eyes on the last rays of the setting sun, as they faded away beyond the distant ocean. The gleam of the twilight hung over the mountain glade for a moment, and the chill night wind swept by as the traveller told Satyakāma how he had travelled far from his camp and now sought shelter. The ascetic sage answered not, but remembering how the tree withdraws not its shade from the woodcutter that comes to cleave it asunder, and how the sandal wood scents the axe that pierces deep into its bleeding heart, he led the stranger to his hermitage, placed

The Dream

food before him, and then showed him an ancient ruined monastery that lay close at hand, carved out of solid rock on the mountain side, where he might find rest.

Over-wearied from his long day's journey, the traveller lay awake, wondering over the strange hermit of Mount Kailāsa, watching, as the moonbeams shone through his lonely cell, the dim walls around, from which painted pictures of holy saints looked down with placid faces and dead eyes, while close at hand might be heard the muffled cries of the shaggy bears as they wrestled in wild anger by the rushing waters of the mountain streams. In the early morning, as the damp clinging mist crept through his cell, he wandered forth to view the ruins scattered round, where in ages long past heretic Buddhist monks had built the monastery, so that they might live secure from the fierce wrath of the relentless Brāhmans, who ever sought to drive the followers of Sāgya Muni forth from the land.

The sun had risen high in the heavens ere he reached the edge of the forest, when he saw Satyakāma, seated alone, wrapped in holy meditation.

When the stranger drew near, and prayed that he might learn of the sacred love of the East, Satyakāma fixed his proud eyes on him in cold contempt, for the Brāhmans have ever held the foreigners as very Mlecchas, outcast, impure and abhorred, unable to perform the sacred rites, seek knowledge, or hope for freedom from rebirth, equally with all women, and men of servile caste.

When the stranger further sought

to know if the ascetic sages of India could free their souls from the body, so that they might pass to and fro working strange deeds, Satyakāma grew weary and turned away in silence, well knowing that no such powers were ever sought by even the holiest in his land, and that no freedom could ever come to those who clung to delusive dreams of this world and its passing desires. So when the English traveller saw that he had no part in the ways or thoughts of the East he slowly wandered towards the hermit's hut, in front of which sat Sītā, her hands, stained at the fingertips with the dark henna juice, raised to braid her long black hair which shone in the gleam of the morning sun. As he advanced Sītā raised her head and her soft brown eyes met his.

Rising, she received him, after the manner of her people, as a guest, telling

of Life

him that she had cooked rice, and placed it in front of their forest home. As he ate she told him how for five happy years she had lived by the side of her husband in the village of Achinta, away in the south. When she told of her future, how she would journey alone to the far-off Ganges, bearing the ashes of her husband to scatter on the holy waters, and herself sink to rest in its cold bosom, her voice trembled, and she went to weep alone, for Satyakāma still sat on the mountain edge gazing far away, having crushed out from his heart all memory of his wife and her beauty.

For many days the traveller remained on the summit of Mount Kailāsa, having forgotten Satyakāma and his learning. Often he wandered through the forest in search of the prowling leopard and roaming tiger; often he

The Dream

sat by the side of Sītā, listening while she told her happy stories of the past, or recited the loves of Nala and Damayantī and the sad story of Sakuntalā. When he prayed her to let him wait near, so that he might accompany her on the lonely journey through the forest when the soul of her husband found the rest it long sought, she smiled at his gentle words of loving pity, knowing that he understood not the ancient laws and customs of her caste. She told him that she must go alone, but that great would be her reward in the future. Well she had been taught, and fully she hoped, that, for her love and piety, her soul would in the heavenly abode of the gods eat the sweet fruits of the deeds it had done in the past, and then be reborn, free from evil, able to live here on earth a holy life for the benefit of all living creatures, till

of Life

finally, released from all transmigrations, it soars away into eternal rest, never more to be awakened by sad dreams of separation.

One day, when the sun shone bright while the traveller sat by the side of Sītā, breathing in her words and marvelling at her beauty, a tiger stole from the forest edge, sweeping its tail from side to side, as uncertain and uneasy it watched the still form of Satyakāma, who stood wrapped in his own thoughts, seeming as if he were carved out of stone. Silently the traveller arose and hurried through the jungle towards the tiger, as it glared back angrily at the faint and uncertain sound of the approaching footsteps. In an instant the loud report of his rifle broke the stillness of the mountain glade, followed by the dead break in the whirl of the bullet, telling that its course had ceased.

The Dream

Ere the echo of the sound had died away down the mountain ravines, the traveller hastened back to the side of Sītā, who had fallen trembling to the ground. With tender care he raised her, swept back her long black hair that lay fallen in wild confusion over her shoulders, from which her white robe had slipped, uttering words, he knew not what, of comfort. Soon a smile broke through the tears that hung like dewdrops on her long eyelashes, and as she looked into the eyes that met hers she sighed, for she felt for the first time since she had left her native village that she was not alone.

Neither thought, neither spoke, their hearts beat happy, as the life that made them man and woman broke forth with a triumphant song of freedom, but she shuddered as she placed her arms around the foreigner as if for protection.

When Sītā looked up she saw that her husband, to whom life had once more grown real, had rushed forward, his face raging with fury and passion, to save his wife from the polluting touch of the abhorred Mleccha who knelt by her side.

The veil of Māyā once more shrouded the soul of Satyakāma, and he saw not in his delusion that Sītā had thrown herself in front of the unresisting stranger.

Swift fell the stroke, and deep plunged the knife into the gentle heart of Sītā, who fell to kiss the feet of her husband, who once dreamed that he was God.

* * * *

The wild wind moaned as it crept up the side of the mountain, and laughed in the ears of Satyakāma as it sped to lick up the flames that carried the soul of Sītā to rest. The tiger roared as it prowled round the flickering embers, turning every now and then to listen to the maniac cries of the Brāhman who sat by the mountain side, proclaiming that the world was false, and that he had gained Nirvāna, and the song of the bearers broke the stillness of night as they rapidly bore the traveller down the hillside to seek his camp at the foot of the mountain.

THE CLOUD MESSENGER.

The poem, in the original, is unanimously considered by all critics, European and Indian, to be the most perfect gem of Sanskrit literature. It was composed by Kâlidâsa, the acknowledged Shakespeare of the Indian Drama, who, according to evidence which I see no reason to reject, flourished at the Court of a king entitled Vikramâditya, whose reign commenced at Ujjayinî in the year 56 B.C.

The Text, with a translation in English verse, was first published at Calcutta in 1813 by Horace Hayman Wilson.

THE CLOUD MESSENGER.

(*Adapted from the Sanskrit.*)

DEEP hid amid the holy recesses of the Himālayas lies the abode of the dread god Siva, a city, stored with treasures loved by God and men, guarded by the Yakshas, once kings among mortals.

Of old it is told how, while the appointed guardian, a lordly Yaksha, slept, dreaming of the beauty of his newly-wedded wife, the great Elephant on which the God of the Rain rides through the clouds, broke down the boundaries of the heaven of the

The Cloud

fierce god and roamed in wild rage through the celestial pleasure groves. Then the Yaksha king, driven forth from heaven by the wrath of Siva, took up his lonely abode in the far-famed hermitage in the south, where once the exiled Rāma mourned in sad silence by the side of his gentle wife Sītā. There for eight long months, amid the shades of the forest trees, by the banks of the holy river ever running clear since the glad day when the loved form of Sītā was mirrored in its rippling waters, the Yaksha king, bereft of his power and severed from his wife, pined in sad solitude.

One day in the hot months, when the parched earth pants for the rain as the loving heart pants for the return of a lover, the king, whose sorrow had so paled his cheeks and thinned his frame that his heavy gold bracelet had

Messenger

slipped down from his arm and lay loose on his hand, sat gazing on a dark heavy cloud as it came creeping up a far-off mountain side, like to an elephant hastening to rush in playful sport against a city's ramparts. Long he sat sighing deeply as he remembered how in the long hot days, not only the face of the husbandman shines bright when the rain cloud comes near, bringing joy to the waving rice-fields, but how the heart of a lover pants to beat happy by the side of a loved one. As he watched the heavy, dark, clinging cloud, he longed to pour forth words of love to his wife, telling of his welfare, so that her life might be comforted. With gentle care he plucked the frail forest flowers, and, scattering them to the winds as an offering, spoke trembling words, so that the lingering cloud might waft them to

The Cloud

the ears of his beloved, for oft the soul when pained with love pours forth its woes to the running brook and whispering wind. So he breathed his eager prayer to the Cloud, as if it tarried on the mountain side to drink in the plaint of a lover, his eager thoughts staying not to consider that as it hurried on to the far north, with its heavy burden of thunder, rain, and lightning, it had no ear for his words.

"O heavenly Cloud, ever changing in form, I know thee, world renowned, born in the ethereal mists, great friend of the God of Rain, stay and listen to the prayer of one cursed by fate, for even if your aid fail, I pray to one of no mean power. You, great friend of the weary, you who gladden the dried-up land with your water, bear news of my welfare to my beloved, for the curse of the mighty god sits heavy on our hearts. Hasten on to the heavenly city where the abode of my loved one gleams bright amid the pleasure groves ever shining in the glowing rays that circle round the divine head of the great god Siva.

"Mount quick on the wings of the moving winds, stay not on your path to gladden the hearts of those who, bereft of their husbands, rush forth with new awakened joy, hoping that with the coming of the rain their long trailing hair will be loosened to fall in heavy folds round their shoulders as they welcome the home coming of their loved ones who have travelled afar. My wife sits pining alone, her hair is bound up, she hastens not forth at the coming of the rain, and none beareth news of her beloved, for I wait here the servant of another. Hasten on to her side, gladden her heart. Gently glide on the soft south wind, following the fleeting birds, while round about thy path hover the trailing cranes, stretching forth their long necks in pride as they hasten north to build their nests and rear their young.

"Hurry on to the side of my wife, thou whose path none can stay. Her soul is weary, for when has the gentle heart of a loved one borne up against sad fate unless urged by hope it fades as a flower.

"She mourns alone, my sole beloved, counting the weary days of separation not yet full. But you, O Cloud, travel not alone, for by your side plays your dazzling bride the Lightning, on whose brightness no eye may long rest, and as your thunder bursts forth the stately swans fly from the lotus leaves to accompany you to the far-off heavenly

Messenger

Kailāsa, where lie hid the pleasing waters of the holy lake Mānasa. Quit now thy dear friend the lofty peak, marked on its side by the deep impress of the sacred foot of Rāma, the holy place of pilgrimage of all born in our land. Year by year, as you return, linger for a moment to shed warm tears in sad sorrow for thy long absence. Ere you depart I whisper in your ear my fond message for my wife, and tell the long journey that lies before you, the many mountain peaks where, when weary, your foot may rest, the many flowing rivers whose cooling waters you, when faint, may drink.

" First rise from these hills in whose recesses lie sedge-grown ponds and lonely marshes, float towards the far north, terrifying the heavenly nymphs who, with timid eyes, look up fearing, as thy black form hurries past, that the wind

The Cloud

now hurls the mountain summit through the skies. Drive from thy path the mighty elephants, guardians of the world's eight quarters, drown their pride with the roar of thy thunder.

"Soon athwart the bow of the Rain-god, now quivering in the eastward sky, thy dark side will gleam forth, shining bright with the many tints of rich jewels as when the divine face of the black Krishna sprang radiant from amid the plumage of the peacock's tail.

"Tarry not, vain with your glory, for far away to the west the land smells heavy from the newly ploughed earth, and the soft, pleading eyes of the simple village women, who know not how to woo thee with wanton looks, wait the coming of the rain to the new-sown seed. As you sail on, tarry for a moment when weary on the summit of the high mountain famed for its thick groves of dark mango-trees. Oft has its high peak cried in joy when your heavy rain has cooled its sides, burned deep with the quick-rolling forest fires. Even those who are lowly remember past kindnesses, and turn not from a pleading friend who seeks refuge. Will not the high hill be gladdened by your coming?

"Then the mountain, thick covered with the glowing mango fruit, will shine pale in the mid-day sun, as though it were the earth's vast swelling breast, crowned at its summit with thy dark shadow trailing down its sides like the tresses of a maiden.

"Lightened of your teeming burden, the heavy rain, sink to rest for a moment amid the rude forest huts of the wild hill people, then soar high to the lofty Vindhya, from whose rugged sides spring, like the serried lines down the elephant's dark back, the many rippling streams of the wide-spreading Nerbudda.

"Alight on the banks of the wide river as it glides slowly beneath the spreading trees of the forest, where the roaming elephants sport in wild rage, for if empty of rain you drink not up the sweet waters, the wind, in playful sport, will scatter abroad your frail form.

"As you once more ascend, the new-blown buds, the plantains by the river side, the birds, as they drink in the sweet scent of the forest burned soil, and see the new dark-green shoots burst forth, will herald forth thy course with songs of joy. When in the air your thunder rolls, the heavenly hosts accompanied by their fond, eager wives will echo forth thy praise as they watch the birds drink in the water drops, and count the long lines of circling cranes that sail around thy course.

Messenger

"Still, bearer of my message, delay not amid the mountain tops, wooed by the cries of the watery-eyed peacocks. Hasten down to the peaceful villages shining bright amid the growing rice-fields, for there the stately swans await for long days the coming shower, and the sacred fig-trees grow heavy with the nests of the building cranes. There sprinkle the new buds of the young jasmine in the groves, and cool for a moment with your shade the glowing cheeks of the maidens whose lotus earrings have faded from the hot rays of the sun.

"Glide by the side of the sorrowing Sindhu; her slow waters are slender like the tied-up hair of a woman who mourns the absence of a lover. Pour forth thy rain and fill her with gladness, for even now the gleam of her waters are paled by the strewn leaves of the forest trees.

Then hasten to the far-famed city of Ujjain, founded in ancient days by holy men whose souls, finding not within the boundaries of Heaven a fit recompense for their good deeds, descended again to this world bearing a portion of their celestial abode wherewith to frame here a kingdom equal to their merits.

"The sacred city lies by the deep gliding river whose waters gleam bright, girdled by long rows of birds heaving on the gentle swell of its rippling waves. There the wind echoes with the sweet, deep-sounding notes of cranes; it steals gently on, as the whispered words of a lover, soft as the perfume of the lotus in the early morning, over the languid limbs of those who, dreaming sweet dreams of their lovers, sink to rest. Sweep on past the latticed windows, drinking in the sweet perfume from the dark tresses of the city maidens, stay to watch the peacocks dance in the pleasure groves as they greet thy coming, then rest on the palace roofs stained here and there by the red dye from the damp feet of the dancing girls.

" But tarry not long, speed on thy way towards the abode of the great god Siva, the dread ruler of the three worlds, there his attendant hosts will bow down before thee, dreaming that they see in thy blue tint the dark stain on the neck of their lord, received when he drank up the flaming poison as it crept forth over the land when the great waters receded after the deluge. The pleasure gardens or the heavenly home are gently swayed by winds sweet-smelling with the lotus pollen, blowing cool over the fragrant streams where sport the heavenly nymphs. Ever, O Bearer of the rain, as you approach these happy realms, stay so long as the rays of the warm sun beat across your

The Cloud

path, for if in the evening service of the mighty Siva your thunder rolls forth in the many temples like the peal of the loud sounding drum, great will be your reward. The dancing girls, eager for thy waterdrops falling gentle as the sweet touch of a lover's hand, will hurry forth to greet thee, their black eyes gleaming like long rows of bees, their hands weary with waving the heavy fans deep inlaid with rich jewels, their girdles tinkling to the quick dancing of their feet. When the evening sky lights up your side with the red crimson of the deep coloured rose, spread then like a halo round the outstretched arms of the forest trees, pass not on till the dancing girls have ceased their song of welcome, and the hands of the Great God have forgotten to draw round his form the blood-stained robe from which his beloved wife has ever shrunk in wild terror.

Messenger

Let thy lightning, like the running streak on the goldsmith's touchstone, gleam forth with wild glee as it pierces the black darkness that strikes fear to the hearts of those who steal in secret to their lovers; drive them not back with thy rolling thunder and heavy rain. Rest then for the night by the side of thy spouse the Lightning, she will be weary from her loving play. But soon as the first rays of the sun move the morning air, rise and hurry on with thy message, stay not in the path of the sun, as it comes to gladden the hearts of those who mourn through the long night, and to dry up the heavy tears glistening on the lotus leaves.

" As you sail on let thy shadow sink deep into the waters of the Gambhīra as it sparkles with the gleam of its glistening gold fish, let not her glance, clear as the lotus flower, fall on your heart in vain.

Strip from off her rolling sides her covering of blue water, held there by her tender hands the long trailing reeds; but tarry not to drink in the beauty of her form, else you may there sink to rest forgetful of my beloved who mourns alone.

"The wind, cool as it floats over the new-ploughed damp earth, will waft thee over the lofty mountains, where the elephants await with raised trunks the coming rain. Make the peacocks, whose eyes shine white in the rays of the crescent moon that rests on the head of Siva, dance as they hear the heavy roll of thy thunder echo on the hill tops.

"Bow down as you approach the battle-field of the dread god of war; be not angry if the heavenly minstrels, fearing thy waterdrops, tune not their Vinas, from afar they watch in wondering silence thy bright form shine as a sapphire in the midst of the broad river which gleams as a long pearl necklace in the far distance beneath.

"Approach near the sacred pass, whence springs forth from the sides of the snowy peaks the holy Mother Ganges, whose wild waves, falling from heaven, once circled amid the matted locks of the great god Siva before they sped on to earth to water the ashes of the hundred sons of Sāgara, her white foam laughing loud at the angry frown of the god's dreaded wife.

"Ascend and circle round the lofty summit of the mountain marked with the foot of the great god Siva; there the heavenly hosts bow down in adoration and there hover for a moment the souls of those who, freed from sin, seek rest as they journey on towards their eternal abode in the heavenly Kailāsa.

"There celestial minstrels sing the

well-known victories of their Lord and Master; the reeds rustle loud, filled by the rushing wind; let now thy thunder roll to swell the song of great Siva's praise.

"Near at hand, nestling close to the mountain side, like a lover to the side of a fair one, lies the Heaven of Siva, round the boundaries of which the great Ganges glides as though it were the woven silk of a maiden's raiment clinging close to her limbs. There the mighty temple spires, deep inlaid with jewels, shining like dewdrops, pierce the skies high as your misty depths. The palace walls gleam with colours painted bright, and blended fine as your coloured bow. The sweet, soft sound of drums echoes through the city deep as your thunder.

"There women fair as thy bride, the vivid lightning, move to and fro bearing gold lotuses in their hands; their tresses wave, bound up with long shoots of young jasmine; their faces shine radiant with the pale lodra pollen. There the nights shine bright, the darkness fades in heaven's clear light, trees eternal bloom, and celestial swans glide to and fro amid the swaying lotus leaves, while on the palace roofs shrill shrieking peacocks gleam bright.

"Steal gently o'er the palace roofs which glitter white with inlaid precious stones and star-like flowers, there, as the beaten drum peals forth its deep roll, the Yaksha kings sink weary to drink the amorous wine of ever-flowing kalpa-trees of plenty, while their stately brides turn their blushing faces from the burning flames set in jewelled lamps and strive to tame the flickering tell-tale light with sand strewn from their outstretched hands.

"But note—the God of Love, dread-

The Cloud

ing great Siva's wrath, bears not there his bee-strung brow. With wanton looks shot from their circling brows, maidens fair bent captive to their will their yielding lords.

"From afar you will see the abode of my beloved. The entrance-door gleams like thy rainbow, while bending low with clustered blossoms, stands the glowing young coral-tree ever tended as a dear loved child by my wife. There the stately swans await the coming rain. They gently glide in glittering ponds within whose limpid waters golden lotuses float tremulous on long stems of brilliant turquoise close by sloping steps formed of slabs of cut emerald. There soon the sparkle of thy lightning will spread over the sapphire summit of the lofty hill, deep girt with golden plantains, rising up from the water's edge.

Messenger

"Steal gently near, O Cloud, the pleasure-grove of my beloved, in the midst stands a mirror of clear crystal, set here and there with rich jewels like young-grown reeds, from out of which rises a golden pillar bearing the sacred blue-necked peacock, wont to dance in the eventime to the gentle music of my wife's tinkling girdle.

" By these signs hid deep in your heart, O Cloud, by the sounding sea-shell and sacred lotus, emblems of the dread god Siva, marked on the door-post, you will know the home of my love now empty of joy, for the lotus sinks sad when the sun gleams not near. Light up her home with the soft gentle play of your lightning, dwell by her side, whisper words of hope. For there she mourns alone, she with teeth like the flower of the jasmine, lips like the glowing red berry, tall and dark, with timid soft brown eyes like those of the young deer, flowing hips and gleaming waist, panting with the joy of life, she mourns alone, she the youthful first creation of the Creator. Second life of my life, she sits silent during the long sad days, her lover being absent she pines away like the lotus chilled by the bleak cold wind. The eyes of my beloved are swollen from long weeping, the colour has faded from her lips by her heavy sighing ; her face, hid deep by her heavy, black trailing hair, lies buried in her hands, she mourns as the moon in the dark weary nights. Seeing thee, her grief bursts forth anew, for the rains bring not back her lover to her side, she falls deep in holy meditation, or in idle fancy wanders through the house, dreaming that I am by her side, as in playful sport she stands before the golden cage of her talking mīna, while it echoes back her whispered words of love. At times she sits lonely with the Vīna by her side, longing to sing the old stories of our race, but as her tears fall fast on the moving strings she forgets the flowing words composed in happy days by herself. Soon wearied with the heavy day, she thows aside her tight-braided locks and seeks for rest, hoping perchance that in her dreams she may see the face of her beloved, but ever her falling tears drive slumber far away. Wait near, and stay your lightning when she sleeps smiling, dreaming that I am by her side. Breathe thy cold wind, scented with the soft rain and young blossom of the jasmine, gently on her faded cheeks, whisper in her ear by the slow, rolling sound of your thunder, these words my fond message.

"'Know me, the heavy cloud, bearer of the rain, dear friend of thy lover. To your side I bear sweet music of his heart. I am the carrier of the flashing light and rolling thunder, hurrying on the travellers to their homes, where their wives lie pining for their lovers who hasten to undo their long, braided tresses.

"'Thy husband waits, bereft of joy in the lonely hermitage sacred as the abode of the exiled Rāma, he longs for news of your welfare, for he knows that dangers creep on all sides round those held dear. Removed far from your side by the cruel hand of fate, his loving thoughts follow yours day and night. His drooping soul sighs deep as yours, the weary days of separation hang heavy by him as by you, his tears bedew his cheeks even as yours, his love follows thee, his body droops and fades with thine. He who oft stole to your side to whisper soft words of love now sends from afar his heart's bemoan.

Messenger

"'Beloved of my soul, thou art ever near, I see thy clinging form in the trailing forest tendrils, the glance of thine eye in the startled look of the timid, frightened deer, the play of thy brow in the rippling waters, the glow of thy cheek in the pale rays of the moon, the gleam of thy hair in the long glistening tail of the peacock, but thou, soul of my soul, art far away. In my dream I see thee, my hands are ever stretched out to the high heavens; surely if the gods look down their tears will fall like dewdrops on the tender forest shoots.

"'But it is not given to us to shorten the days or quench the heat of the sun. Left without aid, O loved one, our heart's desire is in vain. Beloved, be not cast down, ever I live, ever hoping. To none have the gods allotted endless joy or endless sorrow, the course of man's life runs, now up, now down, like the

The Cloud Messenger

rim of a carter's wheel. The Cloud, O dark-eyed one, brings thee tidings of my welfare; be not in doubt from whispered worlds of evil rumour. They tell how love fades from absence of news of one beloved, let, then, this message once more light up your heart.'

"Give this my message, O Cloud, hasten soon back from the mountain summit made sacred by the touch of the roaming bull of the three-eyed Siva, hasten, having banished the deep sorrow from the heart of my beloved, and bear me fond words of her welfare, revive my life now shrunk like the closed jasmine bud in the early dawn. Hasten on, O Cloud, bear news to my beloved, spread thy heavenly rain over the parched land, and may you never be separated from your loved bride, the dazzling lightning."

The Gresham Press,
UNWIN BROTHERS,
CHILWORTH AND LONDON.

www.ingramcontent.com/pod-product-compliance
Lightning Source LLC
Chambersburg PA
CBHW021813230426
43669CB00008B/739